DHAMMA
everywhere

Welcoming each moment with Awareness+Wisdom

Ashin Tejaniya

Translated by Laura Zan

DHAMMA EVERYWHERE
Welcoming each moment with Awareness+Wisdom

Second US Edition, November 2015

This is a gift of Dhamma and must not be sold.
You may make photocopies for your own use or to give to friends.
Kindly ask for permission from Ashin Tejaniya first before doing any translations on this book.
For more dhamma materials and contact information, please visit:
www.ashintejaniya.org

Copyright © Ashin Tejaniya 2011
ISBN 978-0-9835844-2-1

This printing of 3,800 copies on November 2015 for free distribution by:
Wisdom Streams Foundation
www.wisdomstreams.org
info@wisdomstreams.org

To support future printing of dhamma books for free distribution, donations can be made to

Wisdom Streams Foundation
at www.wisdomstreams.org/dana
or by mail to:
Wisdom Streams Foundation
c/o Sajama
2223 Grant Street
Berkeley, CA 94703

Thank you for your support.

Printed with permission of Ashin Tejaniya with layout and photography by Hor Tuck Loon.

May all beings be happy!

Namo Tassa Bhagavato Arahato Sammā-Sambuddhassa

Homage to Him, the Blessed One, the Worthy One,
the Perfectly Self-Enlightened One

Acknowledgements

My special gratitude goes to my teacher, the late Venerable Shwe Oo Min Sayadaw Bhaddanta Kosalla Mahā Thera, who taught me Dhamma and the right attitude for my spiritual development and meditation practice.

I want to express my appreciation to all yogis. Their questions and difficulties have once again inspired many of the explanations in this book. I really hope that this book will help yogis to better understand mindfulness meditation and to deepen their practice.

Finally, I would like to thank everyone who has contributed to the completion of this book.

Ashin Tejaniya

Dear Reader

Ashin Tejaniya's style of teaching and emphasis has always been dynamic, evolving with his own experiences and recognition of yogis' difficulties with the practice. This book is an attempt to capture his teachings at this point in time but Ashin Tejaniya keeps coming up with new and better ways to explain things!

We have collected Ashin Tejaniya's teachings from several sources and contexts to include a breadth of material that will hopefully resonate with beginner and experienced yogis alike. Included are translations from Burmese: The little blue book on the right attitude for meditation and selections from Dhamma discussions and morning Dhamma reminders at the Shwe Oo Min Dhamma Sukha Tawya Meditation Center. We have rounded out the topics with transcriptions of morning Dhamma reminders given in English.

Like the first two books, this book has been produced for yogis practicing at the Shwe Oo Min Dhamma Sukha Tawya Meditation Center. As such, some words and terms used here may not be used in the same way or with the same meanings elsewhere (more in *A Note on Words*). May you find the book to be a source of information and inspiration, from *What is Mindfulness Meditation?* and *Right Attitude 101* to excerpts of Dhamma discussions in *In a Nutshell* and *Dhamma in the Mornings*. Please note that this book is by no means meant to replace the personal guidance of the teacher.

We have tried to translate and express Ashin Tejaniya's teachings as accurately as possible. Please excuse any errors in translation and details that may have gotten lost in the process. Kindly contact us with suggestions for future publications.

Our deep gratitude goes to Sayadaw U Tejaniya for patiently lighting the path of awareness+wisdom and teaching us the right attitude for meditation. May all living beings benefit from the combined efforts of those who have contributed to this process: Margaret Smith, Katherine Rand, Chan Lai Fun, Hor Tuck Loon, Becky Chan, Karen Recktenwald, Bhante Abhayaratana, Bhante Khemacara, Preethi Dissanayake, Sriya Tennakoon, Sister Khema, Cheong Thoong Leong, Sister Mayatheri, Maxine Cheong, SSW, Albert Lee, Susa Talan, Alexis Santos, Steve Armstrong, Nancy Zan, Yopi Sutedjo, Hirok Ghosh, Sister Co Minh, Zaw Minn Oo, 1-2, Ma Thet, Walter Köchli, the publishing teams, and anyone unintentionally left off here!

Laura Zan
Translator & Compiler

A Note on Words

We work within the limits of language and concepts to describe and give suggestions for a process of clear seeing that is at times difficult to pin down with words. As such, when reading this book, please don't adhere tightly to dictionary definitions or rules of grammar.

You may notice a new combination word "awareness+wisdom" in the title and in parts of the book. It is Ashin Tejaniya's way of underscoring the need for more than mere awareness in *vipassanā*. Awareness alone is not enough; wisdom must also be present with the awareness on this path of learning and understanding.

Constructs like "the mind is knowing" (versus "the mind knows") are used in instances where it seems more appropriate to describe something in process. The following words are used interchangeably: *watching*, *being aware*, *observing*, *being mindful*, and *paying attention*. Finally, "*Dhamma*" with a big "D" refers to the teachings of the Buddha, the practice of meditation while "*dhamma*" with a little "d" refers to natural phenomena, natural law, or object.

Pāli and English words have been used in combination throughout the book.

Sometimes the English translation is only an approximate, short description of the actual Pāli meanings, but the explanation should be adequate for the practice of mindfulness meditation. Do refer to the glossary of Pāli terms at the end of book and consult Buddhist dictionaries and texts for more complete definitions. "Try to get a 'feel' for Pāli terms when you hear them; try to understand them in context" is advice we will repeat here from Ashin Tejaniya's book *Awareness Alone is not Enough.*

Finally, in order not to have to decide on the use of "she" or "he" in describing yogis' experiences (as well as the use of "we" or "you" in the explanations), we have given a fair chance to each of these concepts. ☺

Contents

Acknowledgements, *4*

Dear Reader, *5*

A Note on Words, *7*

What is Mindfulness Meditation?, *15*

   How do you know that there is a mind?, *16*

   Persistence, *17*

   Who is meditating?, *18*

   What are objects?, *21*

   Start with any object, *24*

   Use any object to develop awareness, *25*

   The mind has to be alert and interested, *27*

   What is a good time for meditation?, *27*

   Waiting and watching with intelligence, *28*

   Awareness alone is not enough, *29*

   Thinking while practicing, *31*

   Know whatever is happening, *34*

   Study everything that happens, *35*

Five spiritual faculties (Indriya), *36*

Sati, *37*

   Turning the mind inward, *39*

   Meditation begins when you wake up, *40*

Samādhi, *40*

   Two kinds of samādhi, *41*

   Wisdom samādhi begins with wisdom, *43*

Viriya, *43*

   Practice in a relaxed way,
     but don't stop practicing, *46*

Saddhā, *47*

   Take interest in your work, *49*

Paññā, *51*

   Right attitude, *51*

   The mind is an aspect of nature, *53*

Pain and discomfort, *54*

Sitting, walking, and daily activities
   in brief, *55*

Thoughts, *57*
Why do we practice the whole time?, *57*

Dhamma Investigation in Practice, *60*

The pendulum, *60*
Interest and inquiry, *63*
Seven factors of enlightenment, *63*
The role of awareness, *65*
Don't let anger grow, *66*
Moha is darkness, *68*
Stir things up a little, *69*

Recap: Questions from "What is Mindfulness Meditation?", *72*

Right Attitude 101, *74*

What is the right attitude for meditation?, *74*
How are we observing?, *75*
Why are we being mindful?, *78*
Be happy with the awareness, *78*
Do all that is wholesome, *79*
Awareness gains momentum, *80*

Mindfulness Meditation Essentials, *83*

From Moment to Momentum, *86*

Any object, *87*
Check the meditating mind, *87*
Observing naturally, *89*
Sitting meditation, *90*
Walking meditation, *92*
Eating meditation, *93*
Daily activities, *96*
Pain, *98*
Vedanā, *101*
Anger is anger.
It is just one dhamma nature., *103*
Consistent effort, *104*
Awareness gains momentum, *105*
Value of awareness, *107*

More Questions..., *108*

In a Nutshell, *112*

Dhamma in the Mornings I, *175*

DAY 1
The meditating mind, *175*

Curiosity and interest, *178*

Wait and watch, *180*

Lobha is sticky like glue, *184*

Understanding the Noble Truth of Dukkha, *185*

Wisdom has no preference, *186*

This practice is for always, *190*

DAY 2

Cultivating wholesome qualities, *192*

All objects are dhamma nature, *193*

Enjoying the practice, *193*

Taste of Dhamma, *195*

Dhamma in the Mornings II, *196*

Mindfulness meditation is a learning process, *196*

Checking the attitude, *197*

Interest in the activity of the mind, *198*

Understanding objects as objects, *202*

Are you sure awareness is there?, *204*

Don't follow the object, *205*

Vipassanā samādhi, *208*

Expectations and patience, *209*

Being present, *210*

When the mind is interested, wisdom is working, *211*

The benefits of awareness, *214*

On right effort and energy, *215*

On right practice, *216*

The Noble Eightfold Path, *216*

Five spiritual faculties (Indriya), *217*

Craving, *219*

Acceptance, *221*

Appreciate that the mind is working, *222*

Strengthening the mind, *223*

Anicca, dukkha, anatta, *225*

Simple experience, deep understanding, *226*

The chance to practice mindfulness meditation is very rare, *227*

Dhamma is everywhere, *228*

Glossary of Selected Pāli Terms, *232*

Do you know that you have a mind?

How do you know that you have a mind?

What is Mindfulness Meditation?

Let's talk a little bit about meditation. At this center, we practice *Satipaṭṭhāna* or mindfulness meditation on the four foundations of mindfulness (body, feelings, mind, and dhamma). However, before we begin, we need some clarity on *what* we are doing and *why* we are doing it. It's important to begin this practice like we would begin any major project, with an understanding of the ideas and underlying principles behind what we will be doing. We need the right background information and right ideas regarding the nature of mindfulness meditation so that we can practice skillfully. We don't want to start blindly!

What is mindfulness meditation? What is our purpose in practicing? What kind of mind and what kind of attitude should there be when we are meditating? How do we practice?

To me, mindfulness meditation is basically working to transform the mind. Meditation is about cultivating wholesome states of mind, nurturing a Dhamma mind, and bringing out the good qualities in the mind. Mindfulness meditation is *not* work done by the body or work done by objects (what is happening, what is being observed, explained further in the section *What are objects?*).

Objects do not meditate. It is the mind that meditates.
That's why meditation is called "mind work"
and that's why you need to know about the mind.

HOW DO YOU KNOW THAT THERE IS A MIND?

Do you know that you have a mind? How do you know that you have a mind? You can see or observe the mind through its workings/functions e.g. knowing, thinking, experiencing, feeling, wanting, focusing, etc. Now, put your hands together and look at your clasped hands. You know that your hands are touching, right? How do you know this touching sensation? What is the mind doing that you are able to know this? You know because the mind is aware and paying attention to it now.

Do you know that the mind is paying attention and aware? Would you know that your hands were touching if your mind was thinking about something else? No. So you can see that it is not merely because your hands are touching that you know but because the mind is paying attention and awareness is a quality that is a part of this attention that you know they are touching.

Can you shift your attention from your palms to your feet? You can, right? This shift in attention is actually the mind at work. It is the mind paying attention. If you know that you are paying attention, then you are aware of the mind. There is no need to go searching for the mind, as everyone more or less knows it. Knowing, thinking, planning, and intentions are all workings of the mind. It's just not as easy at first to recognize the mind as it is other objects because of a lack of understanding of what the mind is.

PERSISTENCE

What kind of effort do we need when we are meditating? Right now many people know of only one type of effort, which is energetic, forcing effort. However, it is wrong effort when it is motivated by defilements like craving (*lobha*), aversion (*dosa*), or delusion (*moha*). This kind of effort will only feed more defilements in the process.

How then, do we meditate? We use the wholesome (*kusala*) effort and the right effort of patience and perseverance in our practice. Awareness (*sati*) needs to be balanced. Confidence in oneself and faith (*saddhā*) in the practice should be balanced. Effort or energy (*viriya*) should also be balanced. These spiritual faculties, along with stability of mind (*samādhi*) and wisdom (*paññā*), make up the five spiritual faculties (*indriya*) working together in meditation.

> *Insights don't have an opportunity to arise when we are very intent on one object without exploring or investigating what is happening (dhamma-vicaya).*

We can't say we are practicing insight meditation (*vipassanā*) when we are just focusing or paying attention because *vipassanā* is the practice of learning about mind and body processes (*nāma-rūpa*).

WHO IS MEDITATING?

You are not meditating; it is the ideas operating in the background (in the mind) that are meditating. If these underlying ideas are wrong, then the rest of the meditation will be done in the wrong way. Only with the *right idea, right attitude,* and *right understanding* in the meditating mind (the mind that's aware or the observing mind) do you have right practice.

The information in this book, Dhamma discussions, Dhamma discourses, and reminders are all meant to give us right information. We then use this information, what we have learned, heard, and know about right practice, as well as our intelligence during the practice (a type of wisdom) in order for wisdom to develop.

We need right view (*sammā-diṭṭhi*) and right thinking. We also need inquiry and dhamma investigation, which is the investigation of phenomena and reflection on *how* we are observing or practicing, *while* we are practicing. The emphasis is on the need for *wisdom along with the awareness* (also referred to as "awareness+wisdom" in this book) so that the wisdom acquired through direct experience has a chance to arise.

The meditating mind, the mind that's aware, or the observing mind needs to be a Dhamma mind, a wholesome mind. We have right meditation only when we practice with a wholesome mind. We can't say we are meditating properly when we are practicing with craving, aversion, or delusion operating in the meditating mind.

When we practice with wanting or expectations, we are meditating with greed.
When we practice with dissatisfaction and discontent, we are meditating with aversion.
When we practice without having a real understanding of what we are doing,
we are meditating with delusion.

A part of the work in meditation is to begin to recognize unwholesome tendencies when they arise. We can't help having these motivations while trying to meditate. We can recognize when there are wrong or unwholesome tendencies and when there are right or wholesome tendencies and their corresponding effects. This means learning what is wholesome and what is unwholesome. To do this, we use the theoretical information we get, as well

as our intelligence and wisdom while practicing to recognize when there are defilements in the mind. We also need to appreciate this process of learning.

WHAT ARE OBJECTS?

We often use the word "objects". What is the meaning of an **object**? An object is *what we experience, what we observe,* and *something that is known by the mind.* There is always something happening so there is no lack of things to observe. They are all happening (or "arising") according to their nature. In mindfulness meditation, we are not controlling our experiences. We observe when something happens or arises, the mind's attention is attracted to it, and so we observe it. The nature of an object is to be known, sensed or experienced by the mind.

In any given moment, there are many, many objects arising at the six sense doors that the mind can possibly be aware of and know.

How many sense doors are there? There are six sense doors! *How we observe* the sense objects is the mind at work. While we need an understanding of the object side, we also need to recognize that meditation is not done by objects. Meditation is done by the mind. That's why in order to practice well, it's important to understand the mind, including how it observes, how it works, and its underlying attitudes. What kind of mind are we meditating with?

When we are focused on an object, we can't see the workings of the mind. When we look through the glasses we are wearing at what we want to see, we may not realize that we have glasses on! Likewise, if there's too much focusing on objects, we no longer see the mind, what it's doing, or how it's operating. If we don't concentrate so much on an object, we may at least realize that we are wearing glasses. That's how the mind works.

That's why I caution you not to focus if your goal is to get a complete picture and to understand the nature of mind and objects. Do you understand? When you practice, the difference between *what you observe* and *how you are observing* (*the act of observing*) will become even clearer. In other words, this knowledge of the object and the mind will become clearer. You recognize for yourself, "Oh, this is object and this is the mind" and that their natures are different. You'll see this as you are practicing. I am explaining this to you now so that you have the information to help you when you are meditating.

Think about this carefully: Are you practicing mindfulness meditation when you sit and focus on an object? Is it mindfulness meditation when you are just paying attention to something? No, that's just focusing on an object. Or what if you are just being aware? What if the meditating mind is full of unwholesome mental qualities?

Let's say you are knowing, watching, and being aware: What is object (mind and/or body) and what is mind, or in other words, *what is being observed* and *what is doing the observing*? Shouldn't you investigate this? Can this kind of investigative quality arise in a yogi who is just intent on observing objects? Can a yogi who's just contented with peaceful mental states get insights into the nature of the mind and body? No. The yogi will just cling to that peaceful state, working to stay longer in that state. There's no possibility for wisdom to arise then.

*So, in mindfulness meditation, we don't need to cultivate
or work on objects or what we observe.
We can and will need to develop how we observe.*

We do this by first noticing or acknowledging how the mind is already observing. Is it agitated or calm? Is there some kind of wisdom present? (More on different kinds of wisdom: *Sutamayā paññā*, *cintāmayā paññā*, and *bhāvanāmayā paññā* in section *Awareness alone is not Enough*). You don't need to try to change how the mind is observing. You do want to take note of how it is observing and the corresponding effects of observing in that way.

Over time, you will notice different causes and effects. When you have repeatedly observed and seen different scenarios, you will begin to better understand the relationship of how the state of mind and the thoughts in the mind affect the way you feel about the object or what you are observing.

START WITH ANY OBJECT

Start with an awareness of any object. As you maintain awareness, keep checking the mind. What is the mind aware of? When it is aware, is the mind at ease or not? Is it relaxed? What is the attitude in the mind? Keep checking. Be mindful that you are not just intent on objects!

While being mindful in walking, keep checking the mind to see whether it is impatient or relaxed. Is that hard to know? No! You just have to keep checking the mind, right? Is it so hard to be aware of the mind? At this point, it's fine to be aware of more apparent mental states and workings of the mind. Don't go looking for anything subtle just yet. How is the mind? Is it feeling at peace or is it tense? Is it tired? You can know, can't you? Observe the mind. What is happening? Here are some things you might want to know:

- With what kind of mind are you being aware?
- How does the mind feel when you are aware of this object?

Try to observe mind-object relationships like this. It is important to have an awareness of these kinds of causal relationships and connections in practice.

USE ANY OBJECT TO DEVELOP AWARENESS

Which is better: Watching the breath or watching the abdomen? Neither is better than the other. They're the same! You should not prefer one over the other. If you do, you are attached to an object.

The object at the nostrils is an object. The object at the abdomen is an object. Sound is an object. Heat is an object. In *vipassanā*, the eyes are one sense door and the ears are another sense door. Can you become aware with any object? Can you start with sounds? Do you have to go looking for sounds? Aren't they always there? You can know that there is sound. Take whatever object is available. There's no need to look for very subtle objects.

> *Vipassanā uses any object*
> *to develop awareness (sati),*
> *stability of mind (samādhi),*
> *and wisdom (paññā).*

A yogi with awareness+wisdom will use any object to develop *sati*, *samādhi*, and *paññā* instead of growing in craving, aversion, or delusion. The mind will grow in strength as you practice with ease and consistent awareness. Remember that the object is not important; the observing mind with the right attitude is more important.

Dhamma practice is mind work, which means the mind has to have awareness.

THE MIND HAS TO BE ALERT AND INTERESTED

Dhamma practice is mind work, which means the mind has to have awareness. It also has to be alert and interested in studying itself. But because of our habitual tendency to pay more attention to what is happening out there, we very often forget to check ourselves. That is why we have to keep asking and reminding ourselves in order to maintain awareness.

Momentum comes from practicing moment-to-moment. We want the kind of mindfulness that keeps going without a break so that we eventually have a natural momentum of awareness. Using a simile, we don't want the type of fire that burns in a flash. We want a long lasting fire from durable materials like wood or coal.

WHAT IS A GOOD TIME FOR MEDITATION?

Many yogis have this idea that their meditation begins when they hear the bell. That's not so! The bell is there only to remind you. The right time to practice is from the time you wake up in the morning to the time you go to bed at night. When you wake up in the morning, check yourself. Is the mind clear? Does it feel refreshed? Is it still sleepy? You wake up but you want to continue sleeping. Is that difficult to know? Can you know all these? You just have to ask yourself.

You are practicing to know the mind and body. Let whatever happens, happen; it is not important. The mind's work is to know and to acknowledge, which can happen *in any* posture or activity. Sitting on the cushion does not necessarily mean you are practicing. Some yogis sit and fall asleep while others sit and daydream away! Is this considered meditation?

WAITING AND WATCHING WITH INTELLIGENCE

In this practice, we don't focus, control,
exert, restrict or interfere.
These actions are motivated by defilements
like craving, aversion, or delusion.

We have very often used a lot of wrong effort to get what we wanted or tended to exert a lot of energy to get rid of something. We've also done things blindly when we weren't sure what to do.

With this practice, you just wait and watch with intelligence. What can you know naturally while you are sitting? You are not focusing or looking at any special object. You are aware and now you observe yourself:

- Are you aware that you are seated?
- What is happening in your body?
- What can you know naturally?

Expanding abdomen, contracting abdomen, heat, sounds…

- Are you aware of your palms touching?
- Aren't your arms tired?

How much effort do you need to know seeing, hearing, heat, cold, touching, or tiredness? Do you need to focus to know any of these? Is that tiring or difficult? See how easy observing is? Would it be tiring to practice like this the whole day?

Ask yourself if you are aware and then begin the sitting or walking meditation. It is the nature of the mind to naturally take up the object it wants and will know as much as it is able to know. Keep checking when you are sitting, walking, eating, or doing daily activities. The mind can know what it wants, can't it? This "knowing naturally" is easier on you. Trying to find the object *you want* requires energy.

AWARENESS ALONE IS NOT ENOUGH

So far, we've talked about awareness and waiting and watching with intelligence.

Remember that awareness alone is not enough!
There has to be wisdom present in the awareness.

Where is that wisdom going to come from? There are three kinds of wisdom: *Sutamayā paññā*, *cintāmayā paññā*, and *bhāvanāmayā paññā*. *Sutamayā paññā* is **information** you get from reading, from listening to Dhamma discourses, or from discussions with teachers. *Cintāmayā paññā* is **intelligence** or knowledge acquired through thinking, reasoning, or intellectual analysis. *Bhāvanāmayā paññā* is **insight** or wisdom gained through direct experience. In short, we refer to them as information, intelligence, and insight. In this book, we may refer to any of these as "wisdom," or be more specific at times by using the words *information*, *intelligence*, or *insight*.

Are you able to work on a certain subject matter if you don't know anything about it? You can perform only with right information. So how do you get right practice? Before you begin to practice, you need to have some accurate and complete information so that when you are practicing, wisdom in the form of information and intelligence are present with the awareness. You need right information and right attitude as wisdom for right practice. The Buddha called it mindfulness and clear comprehension (*sati-sampajañña*).

By having the right information on meditation, you won't run into problems using the wrong information. This information comes from listening to get Dhamma knowledge, asking for clarification, and having Dhamma discussions. I will give you information, and as yogis, you use this information and your own intelligence when you are practicing. You apply these two kinds of wisdom (information and intelligence) to the practice of meditation. Insight wisdom arises when the right kinds of conditions come together.

THINKING WHILE PRACTICING

So, should you think or not think while practicing? You should be watchful of the kinds of thoughts that will increase craving, aversion, or delusion. When people say there shouldn't be thinking, they are referring to defilement-motivated thinking. Of course you can't help thoughts that just arise naturally but you don't help these defilement-motivated thoughts to grow even more.

> *You don't stop all sorts of thinking!*
> *You should think about the Dhamma you have heard,*
> *information you've read here, and reflect on the work*
> *you are doing and consider how you are practicing.*
> *This kind of thinking will help wisdom grow.*

This information I'm giving you now will be working in the mind when you are practicing and you use the theory along with your own intelligence to work skillfully with the situation at hand. Utilizing the good qualities of the mind (i.e. *sati, viriya, paññā*) and applying intelligence is the work of mindfulness meditation.

Question: *There is the object and there is the watching or observing mind. Which is more important?*

Answer: *The watching or observing mind is more important.*

You need to pay attention to the observing mind if you want to understand the truth. Regularly check on *how* you are practicing. Can wisdom arise in the presence of craving, aversion, or delusion in the observing mind? What attitude is the mind practicing with? Check your attitude regularly. Don't be fixated on experiences. They will arise according to their nature and they only serve to keep the awareness.

A wise yogi uses the six sense objects to develop awareness, stability of mind, and wisdom. For those who are not so mature, the same objects will only increase craving, aversion, and delusion.

Question: *Which object is better, the incoming / outgoing breath at the nostrils or the rising / falling motion of the abdomen?*

Answer: *It's neither! One object is not better than another. An object is just an object. If you perceive one object to be better than another object, you will naturally become attached to the preferred object. Later, when you can't pay attention to that specific object, then you may find that you are not able to practice.*

Craving will surely arise when choosing one object over another. Aversion comes in when you don't find the object of your choice. Believing that an object is "good" is really delusion at work!

So, is it your responsibility to develop the object or the faculty of awareness in meditation? Objects will always present themselves according to their nature; your work is to develop awareness. You are not trying to change anything that is happening but working to strengthen and improve the mind that is not yet strong in awareness. Right now, there's little stability of mind, wisdom is weak, effort feeble and faith lacking. Meditation is the work of cultivating and strengthening the spiritual faculties of *sati*, *samādhi*, *viriya*, *saddhā*, and *paññā*.

KNOW WHATEVER IS HAPPENING

Understanding that something is not beneficial is very different from thinking or judging that something is "not good". If the mind labels something as "good," there is craving already. With any object that arises, delusion is already on the scene. Delusion conceals an object's natural characteristics (but not the object itself) and labels it as "good" or "bad". *Lobha* or *dosa* then do their work of grasping or rejecting. So how are we going to meditate? Meditation is the recognition of gross and subtle forms of craving, aversion, and delusion, and all their relatives that are present in the mind while it is observing objects.

> *In this meditation, we practice to know*
> *whatever is happening.*
> *Instead of trying to make the mind still,*
> *we just acknowledge and observe the agitation,*
> *with the right attitude.*

Because we want to *learn about* the nature of the mind and objects, we don't try to calm the mind down or try to remove objects. We don't interfere or control but observe, because we want to *understand* the mind and objects in their natural state, as they are happening. This is right view.

As such, we also don't try to remove aversion when it arises. We are not trying to get rid of aversion. As soon as we try to push aversion away, there is more aversion. Aversion is always negative, having the quality of pushing something away. We are observing aversion because we want to know its *true nature*. This is what it means to meditate.

STUDY EVERYTHING THAT HAPPENS

If our goal is to have understanding, we need to get to know the nature of as many objects as possible, how the mind and body processes work, and the cause and effect relationships.

> *Merely knowing one aspect of an experience*
> *will not lead to any insight.*
> *The data is still incomplete and wisdom is still weak.*

It is important to study everything that happens and to be able to know all objects. So we work with any object that arises; there is no need to create any experience or to keep our attention on one particular object. We need to use our wisdom along with awareness to learn about whatever is happening in that moment. Only then our view broadens, our horizon expands, and wisdom develops. We need a lot of information (sometimes referred to as "data") for this to happen.

Watch out for craving that can arise subtly in the form of attachment for or aversion to objects. Take a step back and observe, using the investigative mind with the right attitude working in the background. Ask yourself these questions: What is happening? Is what is happening good or bad? Is it really good or bad? Is it right or wrong? Why is it happening? Because you want to understand what is happening, you observe and investigate with intelligence. The inclination to know is already there in the mind. The observing mind with the right attitude and investigative faculties needs to be present. So you now understand a little more about the difference between focusing versus waiting, watching, and observing with wisdom.

FIVE SPIRITUAL FACULTIES (INDRIYA)

Awareness (*sati*), steadiness and stability of mind (*samādhi*), effort or 'wisdom' energy (*viriya*), faith and confidence (*saddhā*), and wisdom (*paññā*) are five spiritual faculties that work together in the process of meditation. Mindfulness meditation is the work of cultivating or growing these spiritual faculties to work in balance.

SATI

Sati means not to forget. Sati means to remember. What don't you forget? You don't forget what is right and wholesome. It also means not forgetting the right attitude and right object. To be aware doesn't mean we create awareness out of what was absent before. Sati is about not forgetting—sati is <u>not</u> energetic focusing.

> *The right object for you*
> *is your experience of the mind and body.*

There is only the nature of mind and the nature of body. That's all there is. If you don't forget, you have awareness. If you know what is going on, you also have awareness. So what do you do to have awareness? Most people think they have to *bring awareness back to some object* with the idea, "Oh, my awareness is gone, I must have awareness again." That's a tiring way to practice.

I will give you a simpler, more relaxed way: Remind yourself. When you try to *get* awareness, you may be focusing on an object. The mind that is already thinking wrong thoughts now tries to be aware of an object. That requires focusing energy. When you remind yourself, the mind thinks about the mind and body and awareness is automatically there. If you don't believe me, just ask yourself, "What is happening in the mind right now?" You'll notice

something. What is happening in the mind right now? Is it peaceful? Agitated? Upset? What is happening? You'll see that you can tell what is happening in the mind, even if only roughly. You'll notice that if you think about the mind, the awareness turns towards the mind. That's what it means to be aware.

Turning the mind inward

The mind is used to being aware of external phenomena. We are always paying attention to what is happening externally and especially through the eye sense door.

Mindfulness meditation turns the mind inward. So how does the mind turn inward? If you just think about turning the mind in to what is happening at the six sense doors, the mind is already paying attention internally. It is the nature of the mind to take as an object what it thinks about. Doesn't the mind go directly to your hand if you think about what is happening at your hand? If you ask, "What is happening on my head," the mind is immediately at your head. How much focusing do you need for that?

Another way to turn the mind inward is to notice that the mind is paying attention to external objects. Then let the mind step back to think about what is happening in the mind and body. The mind's attention will be at the mind and body. The body is easier to notice at first because it's more apparent but with practice, the mind will also become easy to observe. I pay more attention to the working or observing mind.

Meditation begins when you wake up

> *Meditation begins when you wake up,*
> *not only when you reach the Dhamma Hall or when you sit down!*

Just think about yourself from the moment you wake up. Reflect on how you will live with awareness. If you think about yourself, you will have awareness. What is the mind feeling? What is the mind thinking? Where is the mind? What is it doing? Use the information you now have and what you know about the nature of the mind. Ask these questions from the moment you wake up. If you are able to do this, can't you practice anywhere or anytime? I began my practice this way.

SAMĀDHI

Samādhi means a steady, stable mind; *samādhi* does not mean focusing. Do we necessarily get concentration by concentrating? Do we get a calm mind every time we focus our attention on an object? Many yogis suffer from headaches and stiff necks because they have used too much energy and wrong effort to focus on objects! It also gets tiring because of exertion of forceful energy as a result of wanting something or pushing something away.

> *Vipassanā samādhi comes from right view, right attitude and right thought which, together with continuity of awareness, gives the mind stability. This kind of samādhi is called sammā-samādhi.*

We can get flustered when we can't rationally think through difficulties in life. Alternatively, we maintain our composure when we can think about a situation intelligently. In the same way, a calm mind develops when there is right view, right attitude, and right thought; *samādhi* can't develop with wrong attitude, wrong view or wrong thought.

Two kinds of samādhi

There is *samādhi* that comes about from concentrating on and paying attention to one object exclusively and *samādhi* borne from right view, right attitude, and right thought. There are two corresponding practices for these two kinds of *samādhi*: Samatha practice and *vipassanā* practice (what we are practicing here through mindfulness meditation). In knowing about the differences between these two kinds of meditation, you'll begin to recognize what you are doing in your own practice.

In tranquility (*samatha*) meditation, the mind pays exclusive attention to one object, becoming absorbed in it over time. Having concentrated on it for a long time (in the right way), the yogi achieves peaceful mental states. However, because of this very strong grasp on one object, other mental faculties don't get used and the mind is no longer aware of other objects it could have otherwise known. There is no investigation of phenomena nor is there a broader awareness of mind and body processes, thus blocking the opportunity for wisdom to arise.

The idea in *vipassanā* is to relate to and be aware of as many objects as possible without trying to create any particular result or experience. Because *vipassanā* is the process of understanding things as they are with the goal of achieving wisdom, it needs an awareness of whatever object or process happening in that moment. Awareness collects data and when the picture is complete, wisdom arises. This openness allows us to see cause and effect and processes from different angles, giving wisdom a chance to grow.

In *vipassanā,* instead of paying attention to one object, we pay attention to the mind, specifically the observing, meditating mind. We check the mind to see if there is wisdom present or if there are defilements present in the mind.

We are interested in whether the meditating mind is operating with craving, aversion, delusion, or any of their relatives because insights can't arise in the presence of these defilements.

So while meditating, it's very important to have wisdom in the meditating mind.

Wisdom samādhi begins with wisdom

Consider an example of two yogis: One yogi is bothered by sounds while another yogi considers them as objects or natural phenomena. Which yogi will have *samādhi*? The yogi with aversion to sounds will become even more agitated whenever she hears sounds, with aversion increasing. On the other hand, the yogi who neither likes nor dislikes these sounds will remain calm and peaceful.

In *vipassanā*, the mind is learning how to not become attached to or have aversion for any object. Wisdom *samādhi* begins with wisdom and invests in wisdom. Because there is right view, right attitude, and right thinking, the mind does not react with craving or aversion. There is no attraction to or aversion for an object. The mind is calm, peaceful, and still. The mind also feels light, alert, and fresh. This kind of *samādhi* is inherent in wisdom and gives opportunities for more wisdom to arise.

VIRIYA

How do you understand *viriya*? **Viriya is the spiritual faculty of patience and perseverance.** I understand *viriya* as persistence, *not* exertion or force! Please

don't wear out your mind or body by striving forcefully when you meditate. Understanding can't develop when your mind or body is tired.

Can you learn something thoroughly if you start and stop the process many times? You will miss the storyline in a TV series if you catch a few episodes and miss a few episodes. Similarly, only if awareness is continuous, where you see the beginning, middle and end, will you then understand the true nature of *nāma-rūpa*. That comes about through *consistent practice*, from moment-to-moment.

Be cool and calm about it. Be interested. There should be consistent effort but not exertion. Instead of using our energy to focus, we use our intelligence and wisdom, by waiting and watching. If wisdom is present, right effort is already there. For mindfulness meditation, we accept, examine, and study whatever is happening as it is. We don't interfere with what is happening. We don't make something unwanted to disappear or stop, nor do we need to try to create preferred experiences. The mind is doing its own work through recognizing, being aware, knowing, thinking about the practice, and being interested, for example. We're just seeing and acknowledging what is happening.

What is happening? Why is it happening?
If there's no need for what is happening to go away,
or what is not happening to appear,
what sort of energy do you need to use?

It's all already here, as it is! You just need to have your wisdom eye open. Just recognize what is happening. If you are not looking for anything specific but just sitting there with your eyes open, seeing still happens. Do you need to make an effort to see or hear? Are you still aware without having to focus on something? Mindfulness meditation is that restful and gentle.

Practice in a relaxed way, but don't stop practicing

What kind of effort do we use in our daily lives? We have automatically used some kind of force primarily motivated by craving, aversion, or delusion. It has become a habit. *Viriya* with wisdom, however, knows that mindfulness practice is beneficial, so we persevere and we know our motivation for practicing. We are running a marathon. Would a seasoned runner use up all his energy from the very beginning? No! He runs at a steady pace, picking up momentum as he goes through each mile. We want this type of dhamma momentum that arises naturally in our practice. It is not a forcefully created momentum.

Practice in a relaxed way, but *don't stop practicing*. At this center, we meditate the whole day, from the moment we wake up to the moment we go to sleep. If we put in a lot of energy or effort, can we meditate like this the whole day? We certainly can't! We'll burn out and probably get depressed. Faith in the practice will go down. That is why we don't exert force; we just use persistence and we don't give up. We keep applying ourselves as much as we can, but we don't slip.

Remember that this is *not* a 100-meter dash. We need to use wisdom effort and energy, *not* craving effort. That is why we do what we can, steadily, but we don't give up!

Question: *When do you start practicing?*
Answer: *From the moment you wake up to the time you fall asleep.*

Is this work difficult or exhausting? No. Just don't forget. Keep checking yourself and how much effort you are putting in. You need to recognize these things for yourself.

SADDHĀ

Saddhā is the spiritual faculty of faith and confidence. You need to have confidence in your practice and you need to have faith in what you are doing. You need trust in the practice and trust in yourself. Be interested in the practice and how you are practicing. More importantly, faith in what you are doing will grow when you comprehend and see the benefits of your work.

Confidence grows through meditation. When you practice, do you find peace or stress? You will never be stressed when you practice skillfully, with wholesomeness. You may get tired or stressed when you aren't skillful yet and practice the wrong way. Once you learn how to practice with Dhamma:

- both the mind and body are at peace;
- you will be free from grief;

- vipassanā wisdom will arise;
- path knowledge (magga-ñāṇa) and fruition knowledge (phala ñāṇa) will arise; and
- the mind inclines towards Nibbāna.

That's what the Buddha stated in the Satipaṭṭhāna Sutta. Right now you are learning how to practice properly. You begin with faith in yourself and the practice. Confidence grows through right attitude and right practice. With new insights, you will naturally feel faith in the Buddha, the Dhamma, and the Saṅgha.

Do you work to *get* the truth or work so that you *know how to practice* properly? Don't think about the *getting* part yet.

> *Instead of expecting results or thinking about end-goals,*
> *take interest in what you are currently doing and*
> *how you are approaching meditation.*

Have faith in your work and learn how you can become more skillful. Trust yourself. How have you benefitted from practicing?

Intelligence and wisdom are necessary here. The intelligence needed for right effort has to come before there can be any *vipassanā* wisdom, *magga* wisdom, and *phala* wisdom. Can insight wisdom surface before any right effort is made?

First learn how to make this kind of right effort.

Between the mind and body, which one is putting in effort? It is *the mind* putting in effort. Can you become skilled in the practice if you don't know:

- the mind;
- what the mind is thinking;
- how much effort the mind is exerting;
- what kind of thoughts are present;
- what kind of attitudes are present; or
- the nature of the mind?

Take interest in your work

Take interest in the work you are doing. Many yogis encounter good and bad experiences in their practice. Sometimes they have good meditation and sometimes they don't feel satisfied with their practice. When I ask them why, they don't know! Do you know why they can't tell me? It is because they don't study or take interest in the work they are doing. They don't know their minds, what they are doing, or why they are doing it!

When you see the connection between what the mind does and what happens, then you will begin to understand the nature of cause and effect. With that, your confidence in the practice will grow even more.

PAÑÑĀ

Paññā is wisdom. **It is *very* important to have the right view when practicing.** It's only when some kind of wisdom is present that defilements are not able to sneak into the mind. So at the very least, the wisdom that must be present in the mind is information (*sutamayā paññā*). This is information you are getting from reading this book, hearing the Dhamma and having Dhamma discussions. The other kind of wisdom that must be present in the mind is curiosity and interest, a wholehearted desire to really understand. So when you are being aware, don't be blindly aware! Be intelligently aware. Applying your own intelligence is a part of *cintāmayā paññā*.

Can a company manager run a business successfully without an overall understanding of how the different areas of his business are connected? He'll make all the wrong decisions using incomplete information. In the same way, we need complete information for wisdom to develop and for wisdom to make decisions. That's why for mindfulness meditation, the mind needs to be willing to relate to any and all objects. The picture is incomplete if we see only a portion of a whole process.

Right attitude

The objects you are going to observe are the mind and body and the nature of the mind and body. The nature of feelings in the mind, the nature of the mind, the workings of the mind, the patterns of the mind, and the characteristics of the mind are all there. What attitude do you assume when you observe these feelings, the mind and/or body as objects?

It is *sammā-diṭṭhi* if you observe these objects of the mind and body as *nature* instead of as "me" or "mine". When you observe yourself, you see the body and you see the mind. What is happening in the body? Do the sensations of heat, cold, hardness, softness, or itchiness happen to you alone? No. Everyone experiences them. Feelings, happiness, grief, comfort, and mental distress are universal and happening in the mind. How can you view them as *yours* when these things are experienced universally? They are dhamma nature, natural principles, and objects. Take them as nature; they are not unique to you.

Take heat as heat, not that *you* feel hot. Everyone feels heat and cold and everyone experiences feelings. It is *very* important to have this right attitude. You have right practice only when you have this right view and right attitude.

> *Have you ever been angry?*
> *When you are angry, and you think,*
> *"I am getting angry," what will happen?*
> *The anger grows.*

Anger grows when you take possession of the anger with, "This is my anger." When people are sad and they say, "I'm depressed, I'm feeling down," then they *really* get depressed. Why is that? It's because their attitude and ideas have assumed the sadness as *their sadness.*

If you consider sadness as just one aspect of the nature of mind, then you'd feel much better. It's *the mind* that is sad, not *my mind* that's sad. It's not, "I want, I'm not satisfied." It's the mind that is angry or wanting. It's harder for defilements to grow stronger in the presence of this right view in the mind. That is why you need to first assume the right view. Awareness with the right view is called *sammā-sati*. You need to begin your practice with this kind of information and knowledge.

The mind is an aspect of nature

The mind is an aspect of nature, not I, not self, no person. The mind is a natural phenomenon. Only when you have this right idea then can you truly be aware. You are practicing awareness to find out about this nature. While you may not understand or realize the right view at first, you can relate to everything that happens with this right view. You can also think through the information you now have.

Why are you practicing awareness? You want to know the truth, the reality of things; that is why you maintain awareness. Do not forget this purpose.

PAIN AND DISCOMFORT

What do you do when you sit and feel pain, aches, or tiredness? How do you observe the pain? If you observe the pain directly, it gets worse! Why? Does anyone like pain? What happens in the mind as soon as there is pain? There is aversion! That's why when there is pain, discontinue observing the pain itself. Don't look at the sensations just yet when you encounter itchiness, aches, pins and needles, heat, pain, or other discomfort. These sensations can become unbearable if you continue to observe them with the wrong attitude.

What should you do first? You need to first assume the right attitude: Acknowledge the pain as a natural phenomenon, as just nature. Only with this right attitude can you then see how you are feeling. What is the nature of the feeling? What is the attitude at this time? When there is aversion, examine the views within your thoughts. Can these thoughts have right view? There is never right view when there is aversion; there can only be unwholesome views.

It is good if you can see and learn about thoughts, feelings, and body sensations together. How are they related? How are the mind and body related? How are the causes and effects related? Your practice is learning about these connections. Just watch and observe. You don't need to make objects disappear and it also doesn't matter whether they disappear or not. Why are you observing? You are observing because you want to know and you want to understand. Observe as much as you can.

SITTING, WALKING, AND DAILY ACTIVITIES IN BRIEF

Can you change your position when you are meditating? You can move when a certain posture becomes unbearable. If you need to adjust your posture, do so. If it's not necessary, then don't move. What is an appropriate time to adjust your posture? I have mentioned before that meditation is developing and cultivating wholesome mental qualities. If unwholesome mental qualities are growing and proliferating because you are forcing yourself to sit still, then you can shift to make yourself more comfortable. Determine what is appropriate based on your own observations.

What do you observe in walking meditation? Start walking, and then ask the mind what it knows. Just ask the mind: What does it know? Or what is it aware of now? You can be aware of walking, sounds, or the movement of your body. How is the mind while walking? If you are too focused on being aware of walking, then you can get tense. How is the mind while sitting or while eating?

It's the same when you are in your own room, or in the washroom. Ask yourself whether there is awareness. Only when there is awareness, then sit, walk, go, eat, or do whatever you need to do in daily activities.

A yogi's work is to:
- have the right view, right attitude, and right thought, and
- be intelligently aware, moment-to-moment.

When you look at your thoughts, don't get swept away by the story.

THOUGHTS

When you look at your thoughts, don't get swept away by the story. It is enough if you are aware that thoughts are happening. I don't advise beginning yogis to look at thoughts for too long or too much as it is possible to get carried away when thoughts can't be seen as objects just yet. Just acknowledge whenever thoughts happen, check the bodily sensations, and alternate between the mind and the body.

> *Don't let the mind be idle for long periods during the day—*
> *keep it working!*
> *Be aware and remind yourself.*
> *Do that the whole time.*

WHY DO WE PRACTICE THE WHOLE TIME?

Why are we asked to practice the whole time? It is because the mind is collecting data through moment-to-moment awareness. When the data is complete, understanding will arise. It is only when we practice consistently and continuously in the right way will momentum build and wisdom grow. You come to this center to practice as well as to learn how to be skillful so you may take this meditation home with you.

Why are we asked to practice the whole time? It is because the mind is collecting data through moment-to-moment awareness.

Dhamma Investigation in Practice

Ashin Tejaniya often refers to dhamma investigation or investigation of phenomena (*dhamma-vicaya*) in his discussions. *Dhamma-vicaya* is the second factor out of the seven factors of enlightenment (*bojjhaṅgas*) and is a kind of wisdom (*cintāmayā paññā*) that we use while practicing. Of the seven factors, the first three factors (*sati*, *dhamma-vicaya*, and *viriya*) are causes, factors that we can "input" or work on. The last four factors are effects: *pīti*, *passaddhi*, *samādhi*, and *upekkhā*. We can't create or make them happen.

The following excerpt of a Dhamma discussion illustrates Ashin Tejaniya's *dhamma-vicaya* in practice.

THE PENDULUM

I was sitting in meditation and listening to Sayadawgyi (the late Shwe Oo Min Sayadaw) giving a Dhamma discourse nearby. Suddenly, I saw this very calm mind change in intensity. The mind that had been quite calm before was now agitated. How did this happen? How did this anger come about suddenly when the mind was so peaceful just moments ago?

The mind was now interested in knowing, so it backed up a bit and began to ask questions. What is happening inside? This interest to know and right thinking (*sammā-saṅkappa*) changed the path of the mind from anger towards Dhamma. Without this right thinking, the mind would have continued along the path of anger and aversion, still believing anger was an appropriate response for the situation.

Did I cut off the anger through other means? No. The mind was interested to know the truth and because of that, it just lightly and gently watched the anger running its own course. The anger was happening on its own.

What was happening in the mind? It was listening to sounds from two different sides. There was Sayadawgyi's voice on one side and people talking on the other side. I was aware of the different objects and the mind going back and forth between the two. The mind wasn't focused only on one thing; it knew a lot of things simultaneously and saw where the attention was going as well.

I then saw this aversion! On the one side, I wanted to hear Sayadawgyi but couldn't hear him well. I also saw the mind talking about the situation and looking for trouble: "How can these people come and talk around here when they've come here for the Dhamma?" Feelings came up as much as this mind continued to talk.

The observing mind saw everything that was going on in the mind. Can you see how expansive the field of view was at this point? After it saw the mind going back and forth between these two sides a couple of times, it saw the dissatisfaction. It was because the mind couldn't get what it wanted, which was to hear Sayadawgyi's discourse. There was this realization at that moment. And in that moment, the mind did not favor one object or another but just remained in the middle. It saw the suffering and just died down. I could just take sound as sound.

What did I realize at that moment? The mind had taken one kind of sound, the sounds of Sayadawgyi's discourse as good, favorable sounds, whereas the sounds of other people talking as bad, unwanted sounds!

I realized then that if there is greediness for something
30 degrees to one side of a pendulum,
there will be just as much of a 30 degree
swing toward dissatisfaction to the other side
of the pendulum if it can't get that something.

No one can block this from happening. So what happens if it's 45 degrees? What about 90 degrees? What if it's 180 degrees? I had realized previously that even before anger arose that the mind would start talking if it liked something. But because of this previous realization and clear understanding, the mind was already reminding itself in this situation.

INTEREST AND INQUIRY

That's how you need to meditate, with interest and inquiry *every time* defilements arise. When you are ready, the lesson will come and you will understand fully. What you want is this understanding, and development of *ñāṇa*.

When I had really good, continuous awareness, I would be fully aware of the object. I used to watch feelings until they calmed or died down. Of course, the mind would calm down eventually. Why? The mind can effectively calm down if it looks directly at something without being able to think about anything else. But no wisdom or understanding arose.

SEVEN FACTORS OF ENLIGHTENMENT

What we need here is *dhamma-vicaya*, one of the causes in the seven factors of enlightenment (*bojjhaṅgas*). The seven factors of enlightenment are *sati, dhamma-vicaya, viriya, pīti, passaddhi, samādhi,* and *upekkhā*. The first three of the seven factors are causes and the latter four are effects. We don't need to do anything to the effects of *pīti, passaddhi, samādhi,* and *upekkhā*. We can't create them nor make them happen.

What we need to cultivate are the causes: *Sati, dhamma-vicaya,* and *viriya*. These are what we can work on.

> *Out of these three, yogis often pay attention to sati and viriya,*
> *forgetting dhamma-vicaya. Dhamma-vicaya is investigating phenomena,*
> *investigating what is happening, why it is happening, or*
> *how we are practicing by using the information we have,*
> *our intelligence, and wisdom.*

Dhamma-vicaya is a type of wisdom that falls under *cintāmayā paññā*. This is needed here. We have to investigate with the desire to learn, to know, and to understand.

THE ROLE OF AWARENESS

The role of awareness is just gathering data. In the incident, there was a wish to know. Awareness played the role of knowing everything that was happening. It knew the mind going back and forth, the feelings, and what was happening.

The answer will come when the data set is complete. It can't arise when there is still some missing data. However, you do raise the level of interest and curiosity in the mind by posing some questions. The solution will eventually come to you when you have enough data for the problem at hand. When mindfulness is not there in full, it only knows gross-level objects. Right now you may have awareness and stability of mind but you also need to go from grosser, superficial levels, to more subtle levels. That is what it means for conditions to be complete.

Sharp awareness can see the inner workings of the mind. The causes that are present can't be seen when there is only partial awareness. You may see that there is no anger or greed present, but with greater awareness, you'll notice that delusion is always present. Yogis sometimes tell me that there is no greed or aversion present in the mind but that is a very surface-level observation. They haven't really seen what is underneath. A strong awareness and a steady mind are needed in order to see more subtle levels. That's what I mean when I say you need to be able to keep the steady mind in check for longer periods. If you can maintain that steadiness (which requires a presence of wisdom) and you ask a question, the answer will come.

DON'T LET ANGER GROW

You too can use different techniques as needed for the situation you are in. Suppose you are at work and there's just too much work going on. What will you do? I would in the past just use awareness. Because there was already *samādhi* available from practice, the mind was able to use that. I had a lot of work to do at the market and it was tough to investigate, so I just cleared out the defilement using everything I had learned (*samatha* or *vipassanā*). I didn't want anger to come up. When I had a lot of work to do, I didn't think about anything else but just watched the anger gently but continuously. It just went down. There was no thinking involved. If I were to think while there was anger, the mind would only think about anger-related things. I didn't think about anything anymore at that moment but just watched this anger for a few minutes and it went down.

Does the anger go to zero? No. You are not free yet at that moment. It's still in there. But you will only see as deeply as the strength of *sati* and *samādhi* present. If the defilement is still there, it'll just come right back up. But of course it's better to handle the defilement while it's still young.

> *When the fire is small, you can just throw some water on it.*
> *What happens if it has taken half the house?*
> *The water is gone, your energy is gone, and so is half the house!*
> *You'll to have to put in something more.*
> *That's why I wouldn't even give these defilements a chance anymore.*
> *I wouldn't allow them to come out.*

The Buddha said, "Don't give defilements a chance to arise." So what are you not giving a chance to? Present defilements? Future defilements? Past defilements? Defilements in the present are already happening. What defilements can you overcome? If you recognize that there is defilement present, you have not reached the stage of overcoming the defilement yet.

If the defilement is happening, it's already late. You are only at the point of investigation. In reality, if you begin to understand, wisdom will overcome it and close it down. That wisdom won't even give it a chance to arise. That's how you overcome it. How does someone overcome it by not letting it in? Do defilements have a chance to arise if there is *sati*, *samādhi*, and *paññā*, and *paññā* is strong?

What if awareness is strong and there's a calm, stable mind, but wisdom is weak? Anger will definitely come up. Some people with *sati* and *samādhi* can sometimes have really strong tempers. Let's say someone has really strong concentration. *Samādhi* alone (without wisdom) can amplify a situation. Defilements also exaggerate situations. Combine the two and you've *squared* it—what an explosion!

You'll begin to look for a way out only when you can't stand it anymore. Someone who lives in the shade will not be able to stand it when it becomes hot around him. So this person will make sure something like that won't happen again in the future. He won't let the anger out although the anger might want to come out.

MOHA IS DARKNESS

If you have just a little awareness, how much will you benefit? Do you see how much more the mind is at ease? It's because you don't know just how much is happening that you don't know how much lighter it could be. There are always subtle defilements underneath. Delusion (*moha*) is *always* there. Delusion is there whenever wisdom is not present. It is only in those brief moments when wisdom is present that delusion is not present. How many times does "I" not happen? Even if you see that for just a brief moment... then delusion comes in to cover it up immediately.

Moha is darkness.

You have this tiny thief's flashlight. When you turn it on, of course it'll light up and you can see. You can only see this small part in front of you but you are probably just satisfied with that. Think about it. You think, "*Oh, I know a lot now.*" What about all that you haven't seen? It's vast. You only know what you have seen but *you don't know what you don't know.*

STIR THINGS UP A LITTLE

If you are able to observe this little wisdom as it is happening, then this wisdom will show the way. You don't realize what you don't yet know. You only understand this little portion. That is why you can't just be satisfied and stop there. It's not enough when you understand something. You don't know the nature of delusion. When do you understand the nature of delusion?

You will understand when there's wisdom. Delusion steps down for a brief while when wisdom arises. Then you'll see just how much delusion is present. That's why I don't just ask about objects. I ask you what you know and what is happening in the observing mind.

You have to stir things up a little to help wisdom arise.
What is happening? What about the observing mind?
Ask every so often.

That's why awareness and some questioning go hand-in-hand. There has to be this inquisitive thoughtfulness along with the awareness. As the mind changes, there's this urge to know and understand what is happening. Only then the mind will be alert all the time. If the mind has a little energy, it'll be aware, aware, aware... but let's say it gets cloudy outside, then you become drowsy! When the mind calms down, you may become drowsy.

In reality, when the mind becomes calm, it's prime time for you to use your prior knowledge and information. You previously couldn't use too much of this when the mind was agitated because things would have just gotten jumbled up. You need to be putting these skills to use as awareness strengthens and there's stability in the mind.

Recap: Questions from "What is Mindfulness Meditation?"

- With what kind of mind are you being aware?

- How does the mind feel when you are aware of this object?

- Are you aware that you are sitting? Walking? Standing? Doing daily activities? What can you know naturally while you are doing these things?

- Where is the mind? What is it doing? What is it feeling? What is it thinking?

- What is happening? Why is it happening? If there's no need for what is happening to go away, or what is not happening to appear, what sort of energy do you need to use?

- Do you need to make an effort to see or hear? Are you still aware without having to focus on something?

- There is the object and there is the watching mind. Which is more important?

- Which object is better: The incoming or outgoing breath at the nostrils or the rising and falling motion of the abdomen?

- What is happening in the body? What do you know? What can you know naturally?

- What is happening in the mind right now? Is it peaceful? Agitated? Upset? What is happening?

- When do you begin your practice during the day?

- What is the mind thinking? How much effort is the mind exerting? What kinds of attitudes are present?

- How are you meditating? Are you practicing the right way? How do you continue with the practice?

Right Attitude 101

WHAT IS THE RIGHT ATTITUDE FOR MEDITATION?

Please check your attitude before you begin sitting meditation. What kind of underlying ideas or attitudes are you meditating with? Do you only want a peaceful mental state or do you want to learn about and understand what is happening? The mind can't be cool and calm when you want certain experiences other than what is happening in this present moment.

*The mind is already calm with samādhi
when it isn't following after or looking for specific experiences.*

There is no need to go around trying to force the mind to know something because it is already knowing. It is the nature of the mind to know objects that are happening. Check your own mind. There is no need to create anything. You observe objects and experiences that are happening through their own dhamma nature. You just wait and watch with intelligence.

No experience is a disturbance or a distraction as all experiences are dhamma nature. What happens in the body is dhamma nature and what happens in the mind is dhamma nature. Nothing belongs to *me* or *you*. Feeling hot is just feeling hot and dhamma nature. We feel hotter only when we take ownership of the heat as *ours* and develop an aversion to it.

Everything is happening because of cause and effect. Our work is to

- have the right attitude,
- maintain awareness,
- use intelligence, and
- be interested.

With Right View and Right Understanding, awareness becomes continuous and has the quality of heedfulness and of not forgetting the right object (*appamāda*). It is *sammā-sati* when wisdom is inherent in the awareness.

HOW ARE WE OBSERVING?

There's no need to go around trying to find the object of choice. In this meditation, we pay attention to the working, meditating mind and to

cultivating wholesome mental qualities. As such, we can use any object to cultivate awareness, develop *samādhi*, and gain insight into the nature of phenomena instead of generating more craving, aversion, or delusion through wrong views and wrong underlying ideas.

Because we can use any object to cultivate awareness, we can start with any object.

> *Please don't make the mistake of thinking that there is a better object out there than what you are currently experiencing.*

No experience out there is better than the present experience. What is important is that the mind is aware and knowing. What is also important is *how* the mind is viewing or observing this experience.

There is no need to go around creating or doing, trying to follow different experiences. Is an object wholesome or unwholesome? It is neither wholesome nor unwholesome! An experience is an experience. An object is an object. Objects will always be there. The knowing and observing are the work of the mind. The mind knows all there is to be known. Here's the more important question: *Is the mind observing with wholesome or unwholesome mental qualities?*

WHY ARE WE BEING MINDFUL?

Why are we being mindful or aware? We practice because we want to understand. We wait, observe, and study what is happening in the mind and body so that we can understand their natures. We are not intentionally trying to make the mind calm or trying to have "good sittings". We meditate to see what is happening as it is and to have the right attitude regarding what is happening (i.e. it is nature and nothing personal). We need to see nature as nature, to recognize objects as objects, and to know what is to be known.

As soon as there is a thought that this experience or object is good, there is craving for it. When we see what is right as what is right, what is there as what is there, then there is escape from craving. However, when we don't know how to practice, the craving can only increase. We are meditating to be free of craving and clinging.

BE HAPPY WITH THE AWARENESS

You will see that experiences are just happening according to their own nature when you wait and watch with awareness and intelligence. Let whatever happens happen. There is no need to be happy or unhappy with what is happening and there's no need to like or dislike any experience. Whatever you are experiencing in this moment is the right experience. Be happy that there is knowing and awareness as this in itself is already wholesome.

> *The mind is not silent—it's always thinking!*
> *You should be happy in seeing nature as it is and in being able to recognize this.*

Knowing that the mind is not calm when it is not calm is *sammā-diṭṭhi*. Being aware of thinking when there is thinking is right awareness. But many times you may want this thinking to stop because you consider it distracting. However, when you greedily try to make it still, it will only complicate the issue and bring about tension.

DO ALL THAT IS WHOLESOME

Anything wholesome or unwholesome begins in the mind. Why is there wholesomeness or unwholesomeness? These wholesome or unwholesome mental qualities arise because of our reactions and responses to objects. All that is wholesome begins with right attitude, right frame of mind, and right attention (*yoniso manasikāra*). All that is unwholesome begins with wrong attitude, wrong frame of mind, or wrong attention (*ayoniso manasikāra*).

Always try to live with wholesome actions, skillful speech, and wholesome qualities of mind. Do everything that is skillful: Give offerings and practice generosity (*dāna*), observe morality (*sīla*), develop stability of mind (*samādhi*), and practice *vipassanā* meditation (*bhāvanā*). Among all of these wholesome actions, the practice of *bhāvanā* is the highest, most wholesome action. So please don't forget your goals.

One achieves *Nibbāna* only when all the wholesome qualities are there. A mind without craving, aversion, or delusion is a mind full of wisdom and such a mind can understand *Nibbāna* (please see book **Awareness Alone is not Enough** for more). It's just difficult when there is insufficient understanding and unwholesome mental qualities mixing in along with experiences.

AWARENESS GAINS MOMENTUM

You want to be relaxed. Is the meditating mind unbiased, open, and honest? When the mind doesn't want anything or is not dissatisfied with anything, it's cool and has the right view. It sees nature as nature. Awareness becomes continuous. At this point, you don't think negative thoughts or say harmful things about others. *Sīla* is strong. The quality of *samādhi* is inherent in the wisdom that is recognizing object as object. It knows what there is to be known. *Samādhi* is present because there isn't a craving for some other experience or dissatisfaction with what is happening.

Keeping *sīla* and developing *samādhi* and *paññā* are the work of following the teachings of the Buddha and continuing the Buddha's Dispensation (*sasana*). Everything is already included in every instance where you avoid wrongdoing and do what is right with awareness+wisdom.

Please check the meditating mind:

- Is there right attitude?
- Is the mind aware and alert? Or is it dull and heavy?
- Is there an interest for the practice?
- Is it aware of only one object? Can it be aware of more objects?
- How many objects can the mind be aware of?

As momentum builds in our practice, awareness will grow in strength. As awareness becomes stronger, the observing mind becomes free from wanting. It becomes possible to be aware of many objects simultaneously and from different sense doors.

Awareness becomes like a satellite receiver that is able to capture many different channels.
There is awareness of the observing mind and there is recognition of whether the attitude is right or wrong.

The mind knows what it is doing. While all of this is happening, it is nothing personal—it is not "my work" or "me". "I" am not aware; the mind and object arise together and the mind is just aware. No one, no entity, no person is behind this process. It is all nature.

We meditate for ourselves. Please continue your Dhamma work with interest and respect.

Learn to not focus, control, create, constrict, or restrict.

Mindfulness Meditation Essentials

- The meditating mind is naturally relaxed, calm, and peaceful. Learn to not focus, control, create, constrict, or restrict.
- Why is there so much focusing? It could be that you want a certain experience or you dislike what is happening.
- Do not create or reject and do not forget to be aware whenever something arises or passes away.
- Where is the mind? Is it paying attention to what is happening within (to mind and body)? Or is it paying attention to external phenomena (i.e. to other people)?
- A mind is a meditating mind when it doesn't have greed, anger, grief, or anxiety in it. You'll only tire yourself by practicing with wanting or expectations.
- Trying to create something means greed is at work. Rejecting something means aversion is at work. Not knowing when something arises or passes away means delusion is at work.

- Don't have any expectations, don't want anything, and don't be anxious, because if these attitudes are present in the mind, it becomes difficult to meditate.
- Regularly check the attitude in the meditating mind.
- We pay attention to and are aware of both the good and the bad. Meditation is accepting whatever arises, "good" or "bad," and observing it in a relaxed way.
- Is it meditation when we crave for what seems good or have an aversion to what seems bad?
- It's not right practice if we try to create the kind of experience we want. We are trying to know and observe what is happening as it is.
- There is something unbalanced or missing in the practice if the mind is tired or miserable. It becomes difficult to meditate when the mind feels tense or restricted. Check *how* you are meditating when you find your mind or body getting tired. Is the right attitude present in the mind?
- The meditating mind is relaxed and at peace. It's only possible to meditate with a light and free mind.
- What is the mind doing? What work is it doing? Is it lost in thought? Is it aware?

- Don't try to find fault with the thinking mind—you are not trying to stop thinking. Instead, you work to recognize thinking when there is thinking.
- Is the meditating mind, the mind that is aware, just knowing superficially, or knowing deeply and thoroughly?
- We are not trying to remove objects. However, we do want to understand the defilements that arise in relation to the objects and keep examining these defilements.
- The object is not really important. The observing mind that is working in the background to be aware is of real importance. If the observing is done with the right attitude, then any object is the right object.
- Only when there is faith or confidence (*saddhā*), will effort (*viriya*) arise. Only when there's effort will mindfulness (*sati*) become continuous. Only when mindfulness is continuous will there be a steady, stable mind (*samādhi*). With the steadiness of mind, you will begin to understand things as they are (*paññā*). When you see reality as it is, then faith and confidence (*saddhā*) grow even stronger.
- Maintain awareness in the present moment—don't revisit the past or speculate on the future.

From Moment to Momentum

hen people think of meditation, they imagine a yogi sitting with his eyes closed. The sitting posture alone doesn't mean the yogi is meditating. He could be sitting very still, lost in thoughts!

So when do we meditate? Do we begin when we get to the Dhamma Hall? We meditate *wherever* we are, from when we wake up to the time we fall asleep. Can't we also meditate in the shower or washroom? Don't just sit and daydream away on the toilet! Remember to be aware at any time, when you are in the Dhamma Hall, on the walkway, while brushing your teeth, washing up, cleaning, taking a shower, reading, talking, hanging clothes, or doing any other daily activity.

Since this is a practice we do consistently over the entire day, it isn't necessary to spend so much energy all at once.

The mind, however, needs to be awake, alert, relaxed and balanced as these mental qualities allow wisdom to arise.

It is Dhamma only when we *learn to* meditate, *are able to* meditate, and *continue to* meditate.

ANY OBJECT

Observe your body now. What do you observe when you are aware without pinpointing a specific place like the nostrils or abdomen? Know that you are sitting, standing, walking, feeling heat, hearing, etc. Do you see only when you look? Can you also see without looking? There is the sound of the clock and the sound of birds in the Dhamma Hall. You can hear these without listening. How hard is it to be aware of all these things? Does it take much energy? You only have to be aware like this the whole day.

Please don't think that one object or place is better than another because one object is *not* better than another object. Objects are objects and they are all just arising according to their own natures. As such, it doesn't matter what object you begin with. Start with any of the six sense objects suitable for you. But remember that whatever you begin with, having awareness and wisdom is what's important.

CHECK THE MEDITATING MIND

When you put on red tinted glasses, everything you look at will be red. With blue tinted glasses, everything you look at will be blue. Observing objects with

It's not what is happening with objects that matters,
but *how* the mind is observing them that is important.

greed or aversion is like wearing these tinted glasses. When the observing mind watches with greed, then the objects will be objects of *lobha*. When the observing mind watches with aversion, then the objects will be objects of *dosa*. The mind can't see an *object as an object* (or dhamma object) anymore.

It is difficult to see this greed or aversion in the mind when you are very intent on watching objects (without seeing what is happening in the observing mind). Is there greed? Is there aversion? It's not what is happening with objects that matters, but *how* the mind is observing them that is important.

Only when the mind observes without lobha, dosa, or moha do objects become dhamma objects.

OBSERVING NATURALLY

When does the mind feel tightness or tension? There is tension when the mind wants something other than what is happening or when the mind rejects what is happening. Defilements don't want to let things be as they are; they want something to happen, they want results, or they want to control what is happening and they'll force, focus, create, or restrict to get what they want.

Instead of creating, focusing, or restricting, we want to only wait and watch. Is there any need to focus if we let whatever happens happen? If we are not looking for anything special or specific, we don't need so much energy. We only need intelligence and interest:

- What is happening?
- How is it working?

If we want to observe how something is working naturally as it is, we also have to observe naturally. That's why I say not to control or force anything. We just let the body do its job while we pay attention to the mind and are aware as much as we can be aware, consistently throughout the day.

SITTING MEDITATION

What can you observe? You can observe whatever object that arises. If the mind's attention goes to the nostrils, you can observe that. If attention goes to your hands, you can observe that as well. Are you going to put your attention back at the nostrils if your attention is already at your hand? No. Working to put your attention back at the nostrils when the mind is paying attention to something else is too tiring. What is the difference between the objects at the nostrils and the objects at your hand? There's no difference!

What happens when the mind pays attention to sounds? (Yogis: "We'll become aware of the sounds.") Are sounds going to bother you? They shouldn't bother you if you just consider sounds as natural phenomena. You just want to recognize hearing if there is hearing.

> *When you initially begin meditating,*
> *you may find the mind feeling agitated, drowsy, or restless.*
> *That's not a problem.*

In daily life, you've accomplished things mainly using defilement-produced mental energy. Here, because you are asked to practice without craving or aversion, the mind initially loses strength and becomes weak. Within a couple of days, as you develop a little more awareness, stability and calm, you'll find the mind more awake. What will happen when the mind wakes up a bit? You will notice many, many thoughts! But don't worry—this is just nature and not a problem at all.

> *Thoughts may only seem like a problem if you have*
> *the preconception that they are distracting you from your practice*
> *and you try to stop the thinking.*

But aren't thoughts also the mind? If you really want to learn about the mind, these thoughts are showing the way. Can you observe this? So why is there an aversion to thoughts? (Yogis: *"There are feelings and emotions that come about because of these thoughts."*) If that's the case, how are you going to view these feelings? Are they a nuisance? (Yogis: *"We'll take them as objects."*) Yes. When you recognize these feelings as objects, then the practice becomes *vipassanā* meditation.

Please don't set your sitting meditation to the clock. If you have determined that you will sit for a set time period, you may begin to worry when you have to break your determination for some reason. The resulting anxiety will destabilize the mind and weaken *samādhi*. So, don't set any special time. It's enough to know what is happening in the moment. It's also ok to get up and walk if it is difficult to sit. Just remember to maintain awareness of what is happening in the mind and body.

WALKING MEDITATION

Walking meditation is just like sitting meditation in that you are just aware of whatever is arising or happening. Let the body go in an easy, natural manner. Walk in a natural way and at a natural pace. Please don't walk extremely slowly.

Don't force yourself to watch objects just related to the body while walking. You will get tense from keeping your attention at your feet for the hour or so that you are practicing walking meditation. Just be aware of the body as a whole. If the mind becomes aware of sweating, know that. If it is aware of the hands, know that too. Are your hands clasped? Are they swinging? You can be aware of all of these actions.

You can also be aware of what you see, hear, think, smell, touch, or feel while walking.

- What is the mind aware of?
- How is the mind?
- What is happening in the mind?
- What state is it in? Is it at peace?

It's good if you can be aware of the intention to stop or to move. It's even better if you can recognize why you continue walking.

EATING MEDITATION

Which one should be stronger: *The desire to eat or the desire to practice?*

Greediness tends to come in as soon as a meal begins.
Observe the mind first.
The eagerness to eat is very strong.

There's a certain high feeling that accompanies this desire to eat. Awareness is either very weak or not present in the presence of this strong eagerness. How is the mind while you are eating? Is it relaxed? Check regularly that you are not eating with eagerness. The wanting is pretty obvious and the mind will

feel a bit tight when there is a desire to eat. The mind is planning the different ways to combine food on the plate. How will you eat? What will you eat after you finish this portion? The mind is already planning the next scoop. So unless you are paying attention to what the mind is doing, you'll just continue down the path of thinking and planning motivated by eagerness.

Don't be so concentrated on the food or plate. Instead, continue to observe the mind while you are eating. More and more, try to recognize how the mind is working while you are eating.

- What state of mind are you eating with?
- How is the mind feeling?
- Is it relaxed? Is it intent on eating?

When the mind is relaxed, you can observe how you are moving your body. For example, you can observe how you are holding the utensils, touching, opening your mouth, chewing, or breaking apart pieces. You can also know different tastes like saltiness or spiciness. You can know any or all of these. Can't you also observe what you like and what you don't like? Is being hungry the same as wanting to eat? Being hungry happens in the body. Wanting to eat happens in the mind and is the work of thinking. Sometimes the mental desire to eat and the bodily sensation of hunger become interconnected. You just want to observe these things and everything that is happening as it is.

DAILY ACTIVITIES

Meditation doesn't happen only in sitting. How do you get up from sitting meditation to go to your daily activities? Please get up and go with awareness. As you transition from your sitting meditation to various daily activities, please do not forget this: Be mindful. There ought to be continuity of awareness throughout the day whether in sitting, standing, eating, going, or doing daily activities, making it harder for unwholesome thoughts to enter.

You can be aware of what the mind is doing as you go up or down the stairs, as you put your keys in the lock, or open and close the door. Do you enter your room with your head first or your feet first? You need to observe yourself in these daily activities. What do you do when you are back in your room? Do you just take your shawl off and toss it on the bed? Continue to be aware of what you can while you are in your room. You can learn from whatever is happening. Every moment is the right moment for meditation.

See all the different activities you can be aware of in your daily activities, from washing your face, to brushing your teeth, combing your hair, to changing clothes. Try to be aware of all these things down to the smallest activity.

Observing these bodily actions may be dominant in the beginning, but it is important to regularly check the mind as the meditating mind is more important than what is happening in the body. Have interest in whatever is happening, and whatever you are doing. You want to know everything about how the mind and body are operating here.

Also see what you can be aware of as you go to bed and as you fall asleep. When you wake up, you can be aware of the groggy feeling or wanting to go back to sleep. This is also meditation.

- What are you aware of the moment you wake up?
- Is the body on its back? Is it on its stomach?
- What is happening in the body?
- What is happening in the mind?

You are using your intelligence and wisdom and continually sharpening them for the practice in this way by being interested in the process of meditation, in what you are doing, and by asking these kinds of questions:

- What is this?
- What is happening?
- Why is it happening?

When you think about your practice and *how* you are practicing, you are basically filling the mind with wholesome thoughts, making it more difficult for unwholesome thoughts to arise. Meditation is the work of sharpening awareness, and developing stability of mind and wisdom. Here are some more questions you can consider:

- What am I doing?
- How am I meditating?
- Am I practicing the right way?
- How do I proceed with the practice?

In the beginning, you may feel a little tired when you are learning how to practice skillfully. Once you know how to practice with the right attitude, both the mind and body will feel at peace.

PAIN

It's greed at work if you immediately change your posture to alleviate a little discomfort! On the other hand, determining not to move at any cost could be aversion at work. Of course nobody likes these aches, sharp pains, dull pains, or itchiness. Aversion will naturally arise in the mind when you observe this pain. You can begin to recognize these reactions at work and avoid falling into either extreme of immediately changing or not moving at any cost.

Is it meditation if you continue to be aware of this pain with aversion in the meditating mind? For example, what happens when you are angry at someone and the mind takes this person's image as an object? Similarly, pain will increase when the mind observes it with aversion. As soon as there is pain, the mind is attracted to the pain and pays attention to it. This happens not because it is a pleasant experience but because it is an undesirable one!

What can you do in this situation? While the pain may be quite prominent at this point, please don't look at the pain just yet. Don't look at this pain directly when there is resistance. *Check the mind first.* How do you see or view this pain? How is the mind thinking about this pain? There are thoughts associated with this pain. The mind will feel constricted and tense with the presence of this pain. It's difficult to live with this discomfort. Try to see the sensation in the body and the mental feelings associated with this sensation happening together.

> *So after you have changed the object of attention*
> *from the pain to the mind,*
> *you can have an attitude of "let it be."*

The mind's attitude towards it can be, "It can pass away on its own, or stay for some time. I'll just observe as much as I can handle and I'll move only when it is not possible to watch like this."

So when there is pain, observe the mind. There's a little discomfort in the mind and it's finding it hard to live with this pain. Aversion exaggerates the situation, making the pain seem stiff, hard, or solid. In reality, it may not be that painful. In the absence of aversion, there are just subtle sensations; the pain will no longer seem solid. Even the initial concept of "pain" may disappear.

In short, there is some wisdom in backing up a bit only when you can't handle the situation. Trying to escape when pain first appears doesn't have any element of wisdom. *Lobha* is only satisfied in shifting positions and *dosa* becomes dissatisfied that it has to change postures. Only wisdom recognizes things as they are.

So you can work so that only when you can't handle the pain will you try to back up a bit, relax, and change your position. When making these changes, do so with awareness—this is also a part of meditation. The Buddha never told us not to move while meditating. If there is a need to shift your body, please do so. Or if moving is not necessary, don't move. There is no wisdom in forcing yourself to bear and endure pain when it has become very intense in the body.

Little by little, you can try to increase the time that you are sitting and you will also find that you are able to sit there longer. Once the mind is clear and cool (with the right attitude present), you can observe anything you want. This relaxed mind, when looking at what was considered "pain" before, will no longer consider it painful. When the mind begins to understand this, acceptance will naturally follow.

VEDANĀ

So long as there is a mind, there will be mental feeling and the presence of some kind of *vedanā*: *Sukha vedanā*, *dukkha vedanā* or *upekkha vedanā*. These are pleasant, unpleasant, or neutral feelings. So long as there is a body, there will be aches, pains, sickness, or disease.

> *What is more important:*
> *For vedanā to disappear or to learn about vedanā?*

So what does it mean to overcome *vedanā*? You overcome *vedanā* when the mind doesn't react with greed or aversion but remains with awareness+wisdom. The way I understand it is that there are no unpleasant mental feelings (*domanassa*) or pleasant mental feelings (*somanassa*) in the mind in the presence of what is happening in the body. The mind lives in equanimity (*upekkhā*) and wisdom. That's what it means to overcome *vedanā*.

Even when we say we want to learn about an object, there is frequently a rejection of the unpleasant object and a desire for it to disappear. We want to make something negative go away quickly and we make an effort to end it. When something positive arises, we try to make it last a little longer. Is this Dhamma?

> *Your job is to recognize any feeling as just feeling.*
> *This feeling is not a person or entity and it also doesn't*
> *have anything to do with "you".*

You practice for this type of understanding and wisdom to arise. When you realize that this is nothing personal, you'll no longer find an issue with this. It is only a problem when you take this feeling as "yours". So please recognize the underlying attitude that is present when this feeling arises. You practice because you want to understand.

ANGER IS ANGER. IT IS JUST ONE DHAMMA NATURE.

Shwe Oo Min Sayadaw used to ask, "How big is your anger—as big as a fist or as big as a ball?" Is Chinese anger stronger than Indian anger? One is not stronger than another because they're the same! Anger is anger.

We are used to labeling anger that's happening in others as "their anger" and anger happening within as "my anger". That's wrong view. While we meditate to understand the true nature of these defilements, we can't learn when we take possession of these defilements as our own.

Anger and greed each have their own specific natures. Anger is rough and has the nature of breaking or destruction. Greed, on the other hand, has the nature of clinging and entangling; greed doesn't want to let go.

It's the nature of the mind to have good experiences followed by bad experiences and vice versa while we are meditating. With wrong views and ideas, greed or anger comes in; with right views, wisdom arises. Our difficulties arise from not having the right background information and not understanding the nature of the mind. It is difficult to practice without a thorough understanding of how to practice. When there's real understanding, everything works out well.

CONSISTENT EFFORT

> *We want the type of awareness that develops naturally from consistent effort, moment-to-moment.*

We don't want this doing, forceful effort that uses a lot of energy all at once, only to slack off when we are tired. When we get some energy back, we may recover from our drowsiness and start to be aware once again. It's *impossible* to develop continuity of awareness in this random way.

Please work toward continuity in awareness. When there is continuity of awareness and the mind is able to see the whole process of what comes before and what happens after, without forcing, the mind will begin to recognize cause and effect.

Only work to be aware of what is happening and what comes next. There is only this work and no other work. With persistence, you will develop a certain mental fortitude and confidence in yourself. Try it out if you don't believe me. You'll experience happiness when you are able to see this for yourself. Where is this happiness coming from? This is happiness that arises from knowing.

AWARENESS GAINS MOMENTUM

When *sati* and *samādhi* are weak and defilements are very strong in the mind, you will not be able to see reality no matter how much you try. Without the continuity of awareness, the mind sees something, misses something, and sees something again. Can you thoroughly understand the whole story if you've missed a couple of episodes in a TV series? This inconsistency makes it difficult to grasp a complete picture and wisdom doesn't have a chance to develop. That's why I emphasize consistent, continuous awareness.

> *You only try to be aware more continuously so that there is a chance for momentum to grow.*

As awareness gains strength, the mind will be aware of many more things and awareness develops a momentum of its own. You don't do the work of being aware of more and more objects.

VALUE OF AWARENESS

When you begin meditating, the *sati*, *samādhi*, and *paññā* that were absent before are now present. Appreciate the presence of these wholesome qualities in the mind. What is the value of awareness? What does awareness remove? Awareness removes and replaces non-awareness.

We meditate because we want to understand defilements. We want to be aware of the defilements that arise as dhamma nature. What is wholesome is dhamma nature and what is unwholesome is also dhamma nature.

We practice
to have the right attitude,
to understand dhamma nature, and
to extinguish defilements.

More Questions...

- What is your attitude? Is it right or wrong?
  - Are you interested in the present moment?
  - Do you want anything?
  - Is the mind relaxed?
  - How much energy are you using?
  - What does the mind think about the experience?
- Is awareness present?
  - How does it feel to be aware? How does it feel not to be aware? What is the difference between awareness and non-awareness?
  - If awareness is present, what is the quality of awareness? Why is it strong or weak?
  - Is awareness continuous?
  - What do you understand because of awareness in this moment?
  - What is the benefit of having awareness?

- How is the mind reacting to the experience?
  - Why is the mind reacting or not reacting?
  - How do you feel when you notice an object?
- Is there defilement present?
  - Why does it arise?
  - Why does it disappear?
- What does the mind know?
- What is the mind doing?
- What ideas do you have about your practice?

In a Nutshell

The following are a medley of Ashin Tejaniya's reflections, ideas, suggestions, and mini-cases for consideration. They have been translated from Dhamma discussions, morning Dhamma reminders, and Ashin Tejaniya's little blue instruction book in Burmese. Since these are pieces taken out of context, not everything may make sense at first glance to yogis who aren't yet familiar with his teachings. Do take what immediately speaks to you and your personal experience and keep the rest for another day. ☺

***

It is the nature of the mind to know. Everyone already has this nature of awareness which we are practicing to nurture, strengthen, and grow. We only need more right practice, without forcing or focusing. The momentum and strength of awareness will develop naturally when we practice consistently, moment-to-moment, without breaks. That is called right effort (*sammā-vāyāma*).

There is a vast difference between a mind that is aware and a mind without awareness. The kind of awareness that comes from energetic focusing lasts only briefly. The kind of awareness that develops naturally from continuous practice is longer lasting and doesn't just disappear because of some external causes.

People come to the meditation center with plans to put in a lot of effort and to achieve as much as possible within a short period of time. That's just the work of *lobha*!

Meditation is for the long-haul, a practice we do for life, without rest until final liberation. We need to learn how to be skillful at running this marathon and learn to nurture all the wholesome mental qualities possible.

We don't "give you Dhamma" here. We do teach you how to become skillful at meditation. That's what I'm interested in.

In your daily life, you can't meditate by forcing awareness or unnaturally putting in extra energy into your practice. You have come here to learn a way of practice that you can apply to your daily life.

When you are meditating, there is what is happening (objects) and what is meditating (the mind).

When you are meditating, there is what is happening (objects) and what is meditating (the mind). If you only pay attention to *what is happening* without paying attention to *how the mind is observing*, you won't be aware of the greed or aversion developing in the mind in reaction to *what is happening*.

You'll begin to understand meditation when you are interested in learning more about the mind and you pay attention to the observing mind. Being skillful at meditation is a type of wisdom and more important than "getting Dhamma". That will come naturally once you learn *how to* meditate.

Think about it: As long as we want to see or experience specific objects, there is still greed. We can't say we are meditating when we are practicing with greed in the observing / meditating mind.

When you first begin, it's not enough only to have awareness. You need to reinforce it with other supports: Think about how you are going to practice and what is happening in the mind and body, for example. There are fewer chances to indulge in unwholesome thoughts when the mind is filled with wholesome thoughts. The mind can't simultaneously think two things. If there is right thinking, there can't be wrong thinking, or getting lost in thinking. Give the mind a job and make it work. Momentum builds from having awareness for longer periods from moment-to-moment.

We need momentum to be successful in all areas of life including education, business, or profession. Momentum is also needed for meditation to grow. But remember that this momentum doesn't come from exerting a lot of energy! If we exert a lot of energy, we will have only wasted that energy by the end of the day. We want a momentum that comes out of practicing steadily, without stopping.

Anyone with gardening experience can relate to this: If you want to grow flowers, what do you do? Do you think, "This flower's certainly taking a long time..." and yank it out of the soil? No! Of course, you water it and you put in the appropriate amount of fertilizer. The flower will do its own job of growing. *You* can't force it to grow. You only figure out the environmental conditions that will help the flower thrive.

Similarly, in meditation, you figure out and fulfill the conditions that will help the practice thrive. That's why I ask you to practice consistently and continuously. When momentum builds up, awareness will be there even if you don't want it to be there. That's why you want to practice steadily, throughout the day.

Most yogis know that they ought to practice diligently. However, few yogis are clear on *how to practice* diligently.

Many yogis work diligently to focus on an object. In reality, we are practicing to properly understand the underlying characteristics of an object. Instead of using only effort to practice, we also need to use awareness along with intelligence to learn about these objects. Only then will understanding arise. When we say *viriya* is needed, the kind of *viriya* we're talking about is *not* focusing energy. The kind of *viriya* that's needed is perseverance. Applying our knowledge, the right attitude, and wisdom is what's needed for right effort (*sammā-vāyāma*).

Meditation is

- practicing to recognize objects as they arise, and
- developing wisdom in the mind that is observing these objects.

It is not the work of mindfulness meditation to make objects disappear. We are not meditating to get rid of objects nor are we trying to see or create experiences in the present based on our preconceived ideas of meditation. We practice to recognize and to understand the nature of whatever is happening.

Knowing what is wrong is very important. It's only when you recognize what is wrong that you will also begin to understand what is right. There is a lot you can learn from what you *think* are unfavorable conditions for meditation. There may be unhappiness or suffering. Don't make judgments that these conditions are bad for practice. *There is no such thing as "bad meditation".* In Dhamma, there is only what's happening. Accept the situation and be aware. It's already good if you are aware of what's happening. However, people pay attention mostly to *what is happening* and just go around in circles as a result of having judged something as "good" or "bad".

There is no need to try to control or restrict your movements when you are meditating. Don't walk very slowly or too fast. Just walk at a natural pace. Do whatever you need to do naturally throughout the day. You are learning and practicing to see how you can better pay attention and be aware of whatever is happening.

In comparing the mind and body (physical form), which one is faster? (The mind!) So, instead of slowing down your bodily movements, practice to sharpen and strengthen your mental faculties so that they become natural.

We can see without looking. We can hear without listening. We can also smell without sniffing. In the same way, we can be naturally aware without focusing, without putting in forceful energy. Once there is a natural awareness, we only work to maintain it for longer periods.

You see things as they are happening. Isn't it considered even better awareness when you are able to see all of this compared to seeing only one thing?

When there is a lot of delusion, it's difficult to observe even one object. As the mind's receiver becomes even stronger, it can be aware of many objects and capture many more channels because the strength and scope of awareness widens.

There is so much arising at the six sense doors in this present moment. If you are able to be aware of as many of these as possible, isn't it *sammā-sati*? So the fact that the mind can see more objects in *vipassanā* means that *sati* is getting stronger. It is harder for *moha* to arise when the mind is knowing with some wisdom present. That's why wisdom needs to be in there along with awareness.

There is nothing more interesting than using Dhamma in daily life.

When you have become more experienced with the practice, you ought to be able to meditate with any of the six sense objects.

Yogis tell me how difficult it is to practice in their daily lives because there are so many more objects outside than at the center. What kind of objects do you think they are referring to? True, there are many more conceptual objects (*paññatti*) outside like cars, people, or buildings. That's what people pay attention to, but only because they haven't understood ultimate reality (*paramattha*) yet. Ultimate reality here is also ultimate reality outside. There are only six sense doors / objects in the retreat center and only six sense doors / objects in daily life.

There is nothing more interesting than using Dhamma in daily life. People don't use the Dhamma that much in daily life because they don't know the quality, value, and inherent worth of the Dhamma. Someone who really practices outside will know the value of this practice as something they can't do without.

You need to modify your ideas about meditation practice: You're not *returning home... you're going back to another retreat center*! Think of your home as a retreat center. Right now, you view walking meditation here differently from walking outside in daily life.

Here in the retreat center, maintaining awareness takes priority for you. Outside, there is a lot more eagerness when the ideas of *my house, my home*, or *my family* are propelling you. So you need to begin by altering the way you see your home. Practice becomes smoother when your views towards your home are similar to your views towards a retreat center. Right now, as soon as you go home, all the tasks you need to do outside already take priority.

This has a lot to do with attitude. When you are outside again, keep checking your attitudes, views, thinking and background ideas. When you begin to view your home in the same way that you view the meditation center, your practice will also work out.

There are so many opportunities to practice generosity (*dāna*) out in daily life. For example, you give way to a person who wants to get past you while you're driving. Isn't that *dāna*? Is it *dāna* only when you offer money? What about giving someone space? Moving over and giving the spot you were going to take for yourself is *dāna*. We are practicing *dāna* whenever we are giving.

When I was practicing in the market, I noticed that people didn't really pay attention to where they were going because they were absorbed in their thoughts or counting money as they walked. We had a lot of people walking around anxious or lost in thoughts. They kept bumping into me so many times that I got upset! (*Laughs*) I had to keep moving out of their way. There was awareness present as I just gently moved over for them. As I kept moving out of people's way, I found myself starting to enjoy giving over that space.

When you start to have awareness, you'll see these things. What about smiling? Doesn't that make the other person happy to see that? What's easier on the eyes: A scowling face or a smiling face? So *dāna* is not just about money. Giving space is *dāna* too. Give what you can, if you can. Of course all of this depends on the quality of mind. If the mental state is negative, there's *nothing* you'll want to give. When mental qualities are wholesome, then it's easier to give whenever someone needs or asks for something.

We practice to bring out awareness and to strengthen wholesome qualities in the mind. We become aware of objects when the mental faculties are balanced and sharp enough to be aware of them. We don't see something just because we want to see it. We only see as much as we are capable of seeing.

Intentionally putting strength into our practice doesn't necessarily strengthen awareness. We'll only lose that energy! Only when there is wisdom combined with awareness will the mind grow in strength. When we meditate with the right attitude and right view, our mind and spiritual faculties will improve, fueling a wholesome desire (*chanda*) to continue practicing.

Alternatively, practicing with defilement-motivated attitudes will weaken the mind and body. We will also get bored with the practice, eventually losing the wholesome desire to keep on meditating.

Why is it that the Dhamma and the practice don't follow yogis out to their daily lives? Why don't yogis sustain the desire to meditate continuously and consistently? It is because many yogis come to rest instead of coming to learn to be skillful in growing understanding. A yogi whose practice is aimed at developing calm may stop practicing wholeheartedly when she reaches that state. On the other hand, a yogi who practices to understand the truth will not rest until she has understood thoroughly. If yogis became skillful in developing understanding, then they could use this practice anywhere.

In fact, when the mind is in a calm, steady state, it is in a position to do dhamma investigation. It's ready to practice with intelligence and ready to study and learn about what is happening. If we don't realize that this is the way to proceed at this point, the greedy mind will just step in and enjoy this calm state, which is exactly what many yogis do!

Why are we meditating? Do we meditate to calm the mind down? Or do we practice to understand things as they are? Tranquility is not an end goal but a side-effect in mindfulness meditation. When we understand dhamma nature very deeply, tranquility comes as an inherent part of this wisdom.

Yogis tend to close their eyes when they want to meditate. Many yogis who have been practicing for some time may not be adept yet in meditating while looking, seeing, and talking, as they haven't had much practice in these areas. Keeping your eyes closed or open is not what is important. What is key is whether the mind is wholesome or unwholesome.

- Is looking the same as seeing?
- Can you see without looking?

Ask some questions while meditating. This interest, inquiry, and curiosity can determine how narrow or expansive the field of awareness can be. If you limit yourself only to our discussion questions, this will only take you so far.

In my early days of practice, I had heard people talk about the nature of impermanence. I asked myself, "Is there anything that might be permanent?" I experimented and looked around... I still haven't found it, although it might be out there.

When you just wait and watch, there is more awareness of objects and awareness of the mind knowing these objects as well. You'll know for sure when there is awareness and you'll also know for sure when awareness isn't there.

First, awareness leads. Then after practicing for some time and many understandings later, awareness and wisdom will arise together. Later on, wisdom leads. It's not so easy for this to happen. We need to gather a lot of information when we are doing the practice of awareness+wisdom.

Why do we have to practice? We practice because defilements are very strong. Just observe your mind. With anything that happens, is greed or aversion already present? Or is there awareness+wisdom? How does the mind feel when there are unwholesome mental states? What does it experience? Do you feel dissatisfied or frustrated by the experience? Or can you accept what is happening as it is? Continuing to practice with wrong attitudes will only fuel more aversion and you may eventually become discouraged with the situation.

When there is right attitude with wisdom, it is possible for the mind to accept things as they are. But do note that while wisdom accepts whatever is happening as objects, wisdom does not accept unwholesome qualities in the *observing* mind.

A yogi who is always watching the mind will notice each time that unwholesome mental states arise. It may seem as if there is a great deal of these states happening. If the yogi views what is happening with the wrong attitude that these are personally happening to him, he'll become distressed.

When awareness and wisdom grow, with the right attitude working in the background, this yogi may even feel joyful interest (*pīti somanassa*) in recognizing these states as they are. Here's an analogy: If a policeman were able to catch the thief every time he stole something, this policeman would be promoted up the ranks. On the other hand, a demotion might be headed his way if the policeman kept missing the thief!

Here, the thief is always stealing something! Are you going to experience objects with defilements whenever they arise? Or are you going to observe with wisdom? Pay attention with awareness+wisdom. Otherwise, defilements will have already taken over the experience!

When you recognize thinking as thinking, the mind becomes clear. The mind becomes clear because of awareness. Otherwise, when the mind isn't aware of thinking happening, it can be cloudy or hazy. Thinking is not a problem when you can recognize it as an object, just like you recognize breathing as an object. You may have heard from others that too many thoughts are not good and you won't get any *samādhi* from it. Don't make these decisions based on objects. What's more important is that awareness is present. If there's awareness, it's good. The objects have nothing to do with you. If awareness is strong, thoughts will lessen by themselves. Even then, we are only talking about a decrease in surface-level thinking.

Thoughts related to what's happening at home or about some unfinished business are primarily surface-level thinking. When these lessen and you see more subtle thoughts, it may seem like there is a lot happening. You may notice a whole lot more thoughts happening at a subtle level! These will seem to have increased. The mind is talking from the moment you wake up to when you go to bed... *it's so loud sometimes.* What does the mind say as soon as it wakes up? "I need to use the toilet." (*Laughs*)

In fact, these are thoughts that can only be seen when *sati* and *samādhi* are strong. The mind is labeling different things, judging, reading signs or numbers, talking, or interpreting meanings. When sati was weaker, you couldn't see the mind at work every time there was contact with objects. You can only see this subtle thinking when *sati* and *samādhi* are good. There'll be many thoughts and they're fast.

Behind this mental dialogue is some idea working in the background. *Lobha* talks a certain way and *dosa* talks in a different way. You can recognize these things. In the beginning, you took the storyline as an object. Later on, when you see the thinking itself as an object, you don't pay that much attention to the storyline. You see the nature of thoughts and thoughts as objects to be known.

We don't get something just because we want it or just the way we want it. We can only get as much as there are causes and conditions in place for something to happen or how much we put into the practice according to our abilities. When we understand this point, the wanting for something or some experience will eventually lessen. It will be replaced by a wholesome desire to become skillful at cultivating the conditions to fulfill the causes through meditation.

For those who are trying to get the Dhamma: Have you ever considered what the Dhamma is really about?

It is not easy to see the mind. When you do see the mind, it's not easy for understanding to arise. Defilements are even tougher to understand. You must always, *always* be interested in the mind and continually learn about it.

The most important ingredient here is having the right attitude: What is happening is dhamma nature, an object to be known or observed. Once there is right view and right attitude present, be diligent with moment-to-moment awareness. Don't interfere with objects! Let whatever happens, happen because it has nothing to do with "you". With momentum, the field of awareness expands and wisdom is sure to follow.

When the observing mind grows in strength and wisdom, it will begin to see the different machinations and variations used by defilements. For now, defilements have all the entry-points mapped out because the mind has been their playground for so long. The emerging wisdom is not smart enough to counter the defilements running circles around it. But there is no need to get upset over this—you can study and learn from each experience so long as there is awareness.

Most people pay attention to concepts (*paññatti*). Ultimate reality (*paramattha*) can't be discerned by a mind with *moha*. Awareness knows that objects are happening or arising, but only wisdom goes through to the heart of what is happening to understand its natural characteristics.

So think about it: If we meditate with a strong, fixed concentration (but without right view) instead of learning about defilements and becoming skillful in thinning them down—it becomes possible to create any experience

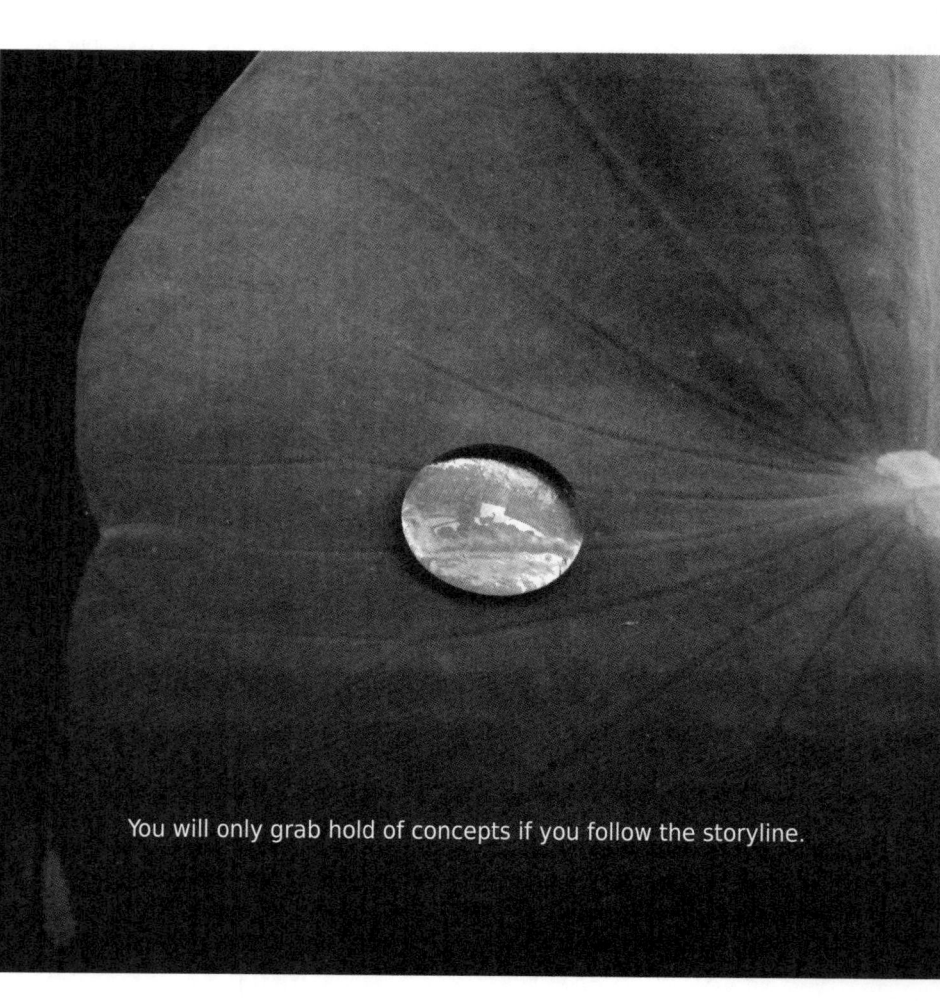

we want! We can create *anything*, even the concept of *Nibbāna*, with strong concentration. That's why I'm so wary of this kind of concentration. It can create anything it wants!

You will only grab hold of concepts if you follow the storyline. The past and future are merely in the storyline. The *nature* of what is happening is the mind and the mind is arising in the present moment. So if you know there is thinking when there is thinking, that's awareness at work already.

Don't immediately assume that the mind is agitated when you see thoughts. There is awareness because the mind has some measure of calmness. Only when there is no awareness can you say the mind is not calm. But so long as the mind is aware of the thinking, there is already some sort of stability there.

The mind can and will create a great many things and will believe the things it has created if it has never seen very subtle levels of mind.

Let me say something here about how perception and wisdom work. You hear a sound. It's assumed that the mind already recognizes sound as an object here. So when you hear this sound, doesn't the mind interpret the sound as the sound of birds, the bell, or crickets? Perception (*saññā*) interprets the sound and creates meaning out of it while wisdom (*paññā*) knows this sound as sound. Do you think this is happening one by one? It's not. It's all included and happening together, in one time. When you are able to see the different parts of the mind working in this way, you can see many things at once. There is no need to meditate on the sound and its concept separately. They're happening together and the mind already knows it.

Are we trying to get rid of concepts? No! Remember that we're not practicing to get rid of *saññā* here. We're only trying to reduce taking concepts as objects but concepts need to be there. Without concepts, we can't even walk or go up the stairs. When we take the stairs, *saññā* has already memorized the distance between each step. Just try adding a couple of inches to the steps we're used to climbing regularly and we'd trip! What we are doing is just paying more attention to reality (*paramattha*).

Saññā does the work of remembering at the moment that there is contact with an object. When there is contact with object, there is already a perception of it. How can we erase this interpretation when it is just a natural part of the mind? Yogis try to just note sound as just sound, sound, sound and it is possible to do this if there is focusing. Yogis can totally lose the concept of "birds" or "crickets" in the process and they think that they are being in the present moment this way. It's actually not the present moment when we lose all recognition of what the object is and any possibility for wisdom to arise in that moment.

A yogi who came to practice with just seeing, seeing, hearing, hearing found that he couldn't practice at all any more once he left the center. Why? We need *saññā* to function. Don't we need to know how much we're selling a product for? How can we answer questions without the use of concepts or if we only hear sounds without an idea of the meaning of those sounds? That's not how Dhamma works.

We know the knowing mind (*viññāṇa*), we know intentions, we know the feeling mind (*vedanā*) but we may not recognize how *saññā* is working. Fewer people will recognize *saññā* at work. Take an example of meeting a person for the first time. Won't you remember him when you see him the next day? How do you remember? You remember because of the work of *saññā*. You'll be able to understand this and see it clearly if you observe the workings of the mind.

Of course if you work in such a way that you focus in on an object so the mind can't think, it wouldn't be able to connect the concept with the object either. But doing that is basically trying to stop a natural process and to stop *saññā* from working. Not being able to think has no element of wisdom within it! There is no interpretation of meaning only because *saññā* has been suppressed but there can't be any further understanding of object and/or mind and causal relationships. Of course, *lobha* or *dosa* can't come in but what about *moha*? *Moha is there in full.*

So, in observing, don't try to break apart the five aggregates of form (*rūpa*), feeling (*vedanā*), perception (*saññā*), mental formations (*saṅkhāra*), and consciousness (*viññāṇa*). Instead, you can see how they are each doing their own job. For example, if you take the roof off a restaurant and peer in from the top, you'll see the boss sitting at the counter, the waiter walking around, the customers having their meals, and the chef cooking in the kitchen. Does each person start his role only when someone else has finished his function? No! They're all happening simultaneously. It's the same with the five aggregates.

In short, mindfulness meditation is not about stopping a process that's happening but about understanding the reality or the truth of that process. People try to stop or cut off processes when they notice a lot of concepts. Wisdom can't arise that way. Wisdom can come in only when there is a clear seeing of mental functions doing their own jobs <u>and</u> *lobha* or *dosa* don't follow close behind. With much practice, you can see the object, how the mind feels, how it reacts, and how it's working. In the beginning, you may alternately recognize objects, then mind, then objects, then mind, etc.

The way you meditate has to change from grade to grade! Are you going to spell words or read sentences the same way in high school as you did in elementary school? Will you still be reading the same way in college? Will graduate school reading be the same as college reading? The way you look at words <u>must</u> necessarily change. Likewise, the *way* you meditate progresses to match the strength of wisdom in the mind. There's no need to go around noting each object by spelling out "c-a-t" but just recognize the word "c-a-t" as "cat".

Right now I see yogis come to retreat the first time and they begin with an object. The next time they come to retreat, they begin back at an object. Is there a need to go back to this level when you can see the object, the feeling mind, the knowing mind, all working together? (Yogis: "We're not there yet.") Do you know why you are not there? There needs to be continuity and momentum in awareness. Because there's no continuity of awareness, there's no momentum and wisdom is not growing. It's the work of the mind that knows object as object, mind as mind, and how they're working. When this wisdom is stronger, it doesn't meditate in the same way it did before. It understands in the one instance that it sees.

My teacher used to say that we don't label experiences or objects with characteristics but that characteristics become clear in the mind. If we *think* about characteristics, then we follow the objects around and think, "This is *anicca*," "this is *dukkha*" or "this is *anatta*". People want to attribute *anicca*, *dukkha*, or *anatta* characteristics to their little bits of experience. In reality, the characteristics of existence are **anicca, dukkha, anatta ñāṇas** that become crystal clear to the mind in an instance of clear seeing when conditions are ripe and no one can dispute that wisdom. These *ñāṇas* don't come about through a thinking process.

Really, "I" is just an idea, a belief. You need to hear about it but realize it for yourself. As you experience it, this understanding will open up to you. I can't tell you a lot about it beforehand. I can only tell you when you experience it. Then you understand and it becomes clear but before then, it's still very intellectual.

Yogis say that the mind wanders outside, or that their thoughts drift towards home and family while they're at the center. The mind doesn't have the nature of "wandering outside," "coming here," or "going home". In reality, thoughts and memories of home just arise in the mind and they also just pass away. You need to have this right way of seeing the mind from the beginning. The mind does not "go out" or "wander about".

If you have the notion that the mind wanders around or goes out, then you also need to use a lot of energy to "bring it back in". That's tiring! The underlying wrong belief that you have to "bring back" the mind that has "gone out" also characterizes the mind as a permanent entity, which it is not. The mind only has the nature of arising or happening. The right way to view the mind is to see that the thoughts are just arising of their own nature. Only through realizing with right view that the mind just arises, arises, and arises will wisdom begin to understand the nature of impermanence (*anicca*).

Experiencing arising and passing away is very different from *understanding* arising and passing away. A person may experience arising and passing away many, many times before realizing anything. What we want is understanding and wisdom. Yogis tend to follow their experiences upon others' advice and immediately think, "I've seen *anicca*." That kind of thought (with incomplete wisdom) ends the path right there, making it difficult for other realizations to follow. Can there be real understanding then?

Note that defilements can also see passing away. For example, a *lobha* mind can see passing away while eating and in effect, wants to eat even more! So can we say that it is "*anicca*" every time we see arising and passing away? Just now, I showed you how *lobha* can also see passing away.

Please don't decide that you have understood the nature of arising and passing away after you've only seen a little bit. That mental confirmation that *you've understood* closes the mind off from seeing more. True understanding will arise when the mind is ready, after many, many experiences. Your responsibility is to cultivate awareness and right view.

In reality, *the same experience* doesn't happen over and over again. An experience happens only once, in this moment. You only think something is a recurring experience because the mind adds up memories of past experiences to this experience. These are all concepts at work (*paññatti*). Ultimate reality (*paramatta*) is always new. An experience arises only once, in this present moment. Your work is to know an experience whenever it arises.

For example, can you tolerate it if one mosquito bites you once? Yes. What if two mosquitoes bite you? No, you can't take it anymore! That's because you're now thinking, "Oh, there are a lot of mosquitoes!" "A lot" or "a long time" are all concepts.

What is more important than an experience is *your understanding* of that experience. Only people who investigate can realize this. You begin with questions like: What is this? What is happening? Why is it happening?

Can there be understanding without this kind of investigative wisdom? *Vipassanā* is a meditation that invests in intelligence and wisdom to develop more wisdom. What is object and what is mind? Do you know this very clearly? You need to recognize this *while* you are practicing. These are the types of things you want to ask, investigate and study with an open, inquiring mind.

Your understanding will be even clearer when you practice dhamma investigation when the mind is calm. Are you just going to be aware of one object? How many objects can you be aware of in one moment? Aren't objects arising at the six sense doors? Try investigating.

If you are only aware of what is happening at the nostrils to the exclusion of everything else, can you say you are fully in the present moment? You can only consider yourself as being truly in the present moment when you are aware of the *nāma-rūpa* in that moment. Can you say that you are aware when you catch one, but miss the other 99? Think about it. Only when you become aware of many things and processes can you say you are aware.

People say that it is tough to maintain awareness. Actually it is not that difficult to have or to maintain awareness. People only think it's difficult when they don't have awareness of their preferred object.

You can have awareness with any object that arises. The object is not important. It is more important that there is awareness in the mind and that you learn how to maintain it. So how do you help awareness grow? You do this by:

- Becoming skillful in the practice,
- knowing how to maintain the practice, and
- knowing how to grow in meditation.

These are the marks of wisdom.

There will always be contact with objects, but defilements won't have a chance to arise when awareness, stability of mind, and wisdom are strong. Your work is to be diligent in strengthening these spiritual faculties of awareness, stability of mind, and wisdom.

Are you yearning for the Dhamma? Or do you want to learn how to practice meditation? *Lobha* just wants Dhamma as an end result. Skillfulness and right practice however, will grow confidence, faith, and wisdom.

You want Dhamma but you don't get Dhamma. Why? It's because what you are actually doing is off the mark. Something is missing or lacking in the practice and it's not complete. The wisdom that understands how to practice skillfully is still fragile. When the type of wisdom that knows how to practice skillfully is complete, then other insights into Dhamma will naturally follow.

If you are putting work into your practice but find that you are not seeing corresponding benefits to what you've put in, ask questions, investigate, study what is happening, and have discussions with knowledgeable teachers. These are ways to become skillful in meditation.

Some yogis have told me that their *samādhi* vanished when they yawned, swallowed some saliva, or shifted around. What kind of *samādhi* is this? It can't be considered stability of mind if it can be so easily disturbed. It's the kind of shaky *samādhi* which only arises when experiences are favorable.

A strong, stable, and continuous *samādhi* develops for someone who has natural awareness of whatever experience that arises or for someone who sees everything as something to be aware of, with wisdom. The mind will do its own work whether awareness is there or not there. Without awareness, the mind will follow orders from defilements. With right awareness, the mind will do the work of wisdom.

A yogi recounted that she thought she was aware while eating only to realize after the meal that she had been eating with greed!

Think about it: How could she have thought that there was awareness when there wasn't? What was happening in the mind? It is because she was not regularly checking what was happening in the mind, but only paying attention to the eating process. It's also because she wasn't paying attention to the meditating mind.

One yogi said, "When I noticed other yogis eating without mindfulness and with greed, I became more mindful. My mindfulness increased."

A wise person will take advantage of an experience to develop *sati*, *samādhi*, and *paññā*. Someone without wisdom will just react to the same situation with aversion.

Our understanding of the Dhamma will grow when we use awareness+wisdom whenever we see, hear, or come into contact with something. It is most important that awareness+wisdom are always prepared and ready for any situation. It's our responsibility to take care of and develop the mind that is able to discern the dhamma nature that is present all the time, everywhere.

How do you sleep? Here, I'm not asking whether you sleep on your stomach, side, or back. I'm asking about your mind. Do you just let go of everything when you fall asleep? Are you thinking? Are you aware? I sometimes like to ask yogis what my teacher used to ask me, "What is the last thing you were aware of before you fell asleep?" Or, "What were you aware of as soon as you woke up?" This is meant to show you how you should be practicing: Up to the moment you fall asleep and beginning again as soon as you wake up. It means that except for when you're asleep, every moment is a time for meditation.

When you wake up, do you realize that you are awake? When do you first realize that you are awake? Do you really know at that time? Of course, yogis wake up, but they don't realize that they've woken up. Many people will just start to do things around the room without realizing that they're awake. *Sati* has not come in yet. Some people may realize that they're awake, but forget again. They only become aware once again when they arrive at the Dhamma Hall!

So here's a suggestion: As soon as you wake up, don't start doing things just yet. Sayadaw U Jotika gave this idea to consciously breathe in for four or five minutes when waking up. The mind will become more alert. Make sure not to do it too softly or else you might fall asleep again! Then, *with awareness*, get up, walk, or do what you need to do. Whatever you are aware of is ok so long as there is awareness.

Awareness becoming continuous isn't like winning the lottery by chance. There are causes and conditions for this to happen. If you find that the momentum of awareness is no longer there, first accept: Everything is nature and this isn't just happening to you. Then check the causes. After many experiences of momentum going up and down, you will begin to see conditions in the mind that make awareness more continuous and conditions that'll break momentum.

People only become awake and alert when there is some sort of discomfort or distress. They stop paying attention once they are comfortable again. Unfortunately, we can't just start practicing only when something goes wrong. That is why the Buddha left us with many notes on heedfulness and diligence (*appamāda*).

The Buddha didn't urge us to be practicing all the time for nothing. It's because he knew about the full extent of *moha* that he left us this instruction. Just try stopping. Try to stop meditation for a while and you'll see the strength of defilements.

If this side of wisdom stops, a party of defilements will just come in and cover everything. That's what I mean by not being able to pause. That's why I also say, "Never give up." Either there is momentum on the wisdom side or there will be momentum on the defilement side. If you were to let go of this wisdom momentum even for a bit, it will take quite a lot to begin again. Beginning again is not that easy. That's why you can't let it stop. Imagine going all the way.

Do you experience happiness and joyful interest when you are observing with awareness+wisdom?

If we are practicing Dhamma every time we are practicing, there is mental and bodily happiness. Insights can't arise in a mind meditating with mental or bodily discontent.

One yogi became really impressed by what she was able to see in just 15 minutes of continuous awareness. Most people are swimming or lost in thought most of the time but it is really amazing what we can discover in just 15-20 minutes of *continuous* awareness. Try it for yourself and see.

You want to listen to my Dhamma talk but you don't want to hear the birds chirping in the Dhamma Hall. You think, "Wow, they're so loud!" This talk is one sound and the birds are another sound. Someone with the right information will use any of these objects to develop *sati*, *samādhi*, and *paññā* in meditation. Another person without this kind of information will only grow in defilements because of these sounds.

Instead of trying to figure out where sounds are coming from, acknowledge these sounds as objects. When you are aware of these sounds as objects, be

aware of the mind that is knowing the sounds. What is that awareness aware of? It is aware of objects. You can stay on the side of awareness or see both the object and the knowing mind together.

When people are going through mental or physical pain, they don't take interest or learn. They only want to escape the pain.

If you have pain while sitting, see the mind that wants to alleviate this pain by shifting. Why is it reacting this way? When this reaction lessens, how does the mind then view the object? You need to study the mind's reaction to pain from different angles and observe the reactions and all their manifestations: How are thoughts and feelings related or what background ideas and underlying attitudes show up through thoughts? If there's even the *tiniest disliking* to an object, the talking mind will change its tone of voice in that way.

You can really get to know this talking mind. Without trying to stop this talking or thinking, you can see the mind's internal dialogue from morning until night. You are observing to understand the mind as it is, *not* to make anything disappear.

When wisdom raises its head a little, defilements just hammer it back down. As soon as you figure out a little bit, the mind is already chattering, "I know, I know." If you want to see the strength of this conditioning, just look at the habit pattern of the mind to say, "I know, I know." When wisdom understands something, the thought, "I know" follows very closely behind. So how can you actually use that wisdom?

That's why I caution: Don't look down on defilements. We don't know just how much they're at work! Wisdom will only have a chance by rising again and again.

Don't think too highly of yourself. Which takes place more frequently: The times when there are understandings or realizations or the times when there are no understandings or realizations?

Awareness does not find solutions. Only wisdom finds solutions. The work of awareness is to know what is happening; this alone can't stop strong defilements; only wisdom is able to do that work.

Moha leaves the door open and all the defilements just walk through.

You can really get to know this talking mind.

When the mind is either liking or disliking a certain object, it can no longer see the object as it is or as dhamma. When the mind is motivated by greed, then the object becomes an object of greed. When the mind is motivated by anger or aversion, the object becomes an object of anger or aversion. The mind can't observe or continue to be aware of this object as it is.

It's like wearing blue tinted glasses whereby anything we look at through these glasses will be colored blue. As such, we can't see the natural characteristics of what we are looking at. That's why we need to first *check our glasses* or check *how* we are observing.

Dissatisfied with what someone was doing, one yogi asked, "Why does he do something this way?" More important is to recognize why this yogi would ask such questions in the first place.

There can be an understanding of anger or aversion as an object. With *dhammānupassanā* and *cittānupassanā*, whatever is being observed (anger, for example) is the object. When we say that there should not be defilements in the mind, we mean that there shouldn't be defilements in the observing mind. There is no way to stop defilements from happening in the mind of a worldling (*puthujjana*) or one who has not yet experienced any of the stages of enlightenment.

But the observing mind can be skillful and free of defilements when it knows how to observe. With right attitude and without defilements in the observing mind, the mind is calm and cool. Wisdom then has a chance to open up.

You need to understand anger deeply. In order to do that, you need to build up *sati*, *samādhi*, and *paññā* and to watch and learn, *every time* anger arises. You want to know the nature of anger and everything related to this phenomenon. What happens in the body and what happens in the mind when this defilement arises? What kinds of thoughts come up? What is the nature of anger?

You (the mind) are an independent observer, studying this anger from the side, as it is happening with the view that this is also dhamma nature, not *your anger* or that *you are angry*. What are the different characteristics of anger? How does it work? What happens in the mind? How does an anger-motivated mind think? You study and learn *every single time*, down to the smallest detail. There is no way for the defilement to intensify if you observe it every time it arises. It can't rear its head.

The bigger episodes will be quite rough, of course, and you may not be able to recognize subtle forms of anger in the beginning. Only when the mind has also strengthened with *sati*, *samādhi*, and *paññā* built up will you be able to see anger from the beginning, *as soon as it arises.* You can say you understand the nature of anger when you understand the whole process of anger from beginning to end.

We need to thoroughly understand how much defilements are torturing and tormenting us. We haven't learned this lesson fully yet. We don't learn our lesson the first time, the second time, the third time... When defilements arise, we just welcome them into our homes as guests, serving them tea and biscuits. Isn't that true? Just reflect on all the things we think about that fuel anger. We'll only turn for help from wholesome qualities when we can no longer stand these defilements.

We like to feed defilements to make them stronger whenever they arise. We don't want heat, but we pour gasoline on a fire! We're supposed to throw on water but we only have this little water-gun children use during the Water Festival.

Without enough wisdom, people try to suppress defilements with *samādhi*.

There are two means by which defilements go:

    1) You become aware of a defilement and it goes away, or
    2) an understanding arises about the defilement.

When you become aware of a defilement as an object, it dissipates from the strength of awareness. Alternatively, there is a realization about the defilement and it disappears, similar to light replacing darkness.

There are latent, deeply embedded underlying ideas that will only surface when you come in contact with different experiences. When faced with that experience, the mind starts talking, motivated by certain background ideas. Only deep understanding will get to the level of these long-held ideas. If these ideas have been held really vigorously before, the present level of understanding and wisdom may comprehend the situation but is not sufficient to really let go of the idea itself.

When something happens, what is more powerful: Defilements or wisdom? Defilements that have come in unconsciously are quite potent and often invisible, having gone deep into the mind. How powerful is something with that pull and that has been inside for that long?

I asked this question at a retreat in Singapore: "So now that you are talking Dhamma, how much greed do you have?" The yogis checked their minds and found that there wasn't anything they wanted in that moment. I suggested that something was there and yet it was so powerful that they couldn't see it.

What kind of craving was I talking about? It's the craving for everything to go smoothly on retreat and elsewhere. Is it possible to see that kind of *lobha*? They were very surprised! There would have been conflicts had we stopped the discussion at that moment.

The type of pull that has been with us for a lifetime is extremely strong, buried in the unconscious and no longer at surface level. Called *anusaya*, such defilements only appear under varying circumstances and *vipassanā ñāṇa* alone can't access this deep level. Only a very powerful *magga-ñāṇa* is able to handle this.

What do I mean when I say you need to be "collecting data"? It means you are observing what is happening *every time* it happens. There are various ways that aversion can play out. If you have awareness every single time that there is this experience and you wait patiently and observe, you are collecting data. A defilement like aversion can be very strong sometimes, while feeble at other times. Why is that? You may not know the answer until your data is complete.

Do you think something is "good" or "bad"? Or do you have a real understanding that something is good or bad? Real understanding rejects what you once perceived as good or bad and just sees it as it is. Understanding also removes wrong concepts about something.

There is a lot of delusion when people are healthy. People only begin to pay attention when they get sick.

It is not important for aches and pains (objects) to disappear. You want to learn about the mind and body processes that arise and pass away in the presence of these aches and pains.

Instead of trying to stop drowsiness, you want to learn about *the nature* of drowsiness. These are two different motivations. You may find that if there's an aversion to this drowsiness, it'll slowly get stronger and you may fall asleep. If however, you are interested in what is happening, the mind will become alert once again.

There are some possible reasons (among others) for this drowsiness:

1) You may have eaten too much and are sleepy,
2) you are not interested in the meditation work you are doing and there's boredom, or
3) it is a habit to fall asleep as soon as you close your eyes.

Be interested in whatever is happening!

Yogis tend to tell me that something is "good" or "bad". Or they'll come and ask me whether what happened to them was good. Please don't take an experience as "good" or "bad". It's only good if you understand more about the nature of what has happened, its causes and effects, whether it was wholesome or unwholesome and the value of the experience.

Please reflect on this: Is there *any* object worthy of greed or anger? Do you truly recognize that craving, aversion, and delusion (and all their relatives) are all unwholesome mental states? Have you really understood that *sati*, *samādhi*, *paññā*, *mettā*, *karuṇā*, *muditā*, and *upekkhā* are wholesome mental states? If you want to understand, please learn about all these with awareness+wisdom.

Kusala has the power to break down the *akusala* qualities in the mind and vice versa. That is why you need to try to do everything that's wholesome including using wholesome speech and doing things with a wholesome motivation. But the highest, most meaningful action is doing things with wisdom. When awareness+wisdom are present within an action, the mind understands how to do things skillfully so that both sides will benefit. Just seeing one side (i.e. let *me* have this, but not others, or let *me* be successful) is the work of strong defilements. Wisdom is the opposite, seeing the same thing *moha* would normally see, in a completely different light.

If we only pay attention to objects, that is only half the picture and understanding will be incomplete. Our field of awareness must expand to include objects, the observing mind, feelings and more. This expanded field

In this world, there is only mind and objects.

of awareness comes about from waiting and watching with patience and intelligence, *not* from focusing on objects in hopes of seeing something. That is why this expanded awareness is so important.

Wisdom steps aside as a detached observer to the entire process that is happening on its own. On the other hand, focusing as a way of observing has more of a feeling of sticking to an object. So of course, the field of awareness would be very narrow. That is why I remind you to neither force nor focus.

We pay more attention to the observing mind than to objects. Is the mind reacting with defilements over this object? We also pay special attention to the meditating mind when the objects are defilements. Are there also defilements in the meditating mind? In this world, there is only mind and objects.

You can no longer see the mind when there is too much focusing. Focusing uses concepts like distance and place. *What* are you going to focus on and *where* are you going to focus to see the mind? By focusing, you will only see the object side. You can only observe the workings of the mind if you are able to wait and watch.

When you open your eyes, do you recognize that there's seeing happening? What is the difference between looking and seeing? Looking requires directing attention to an external object but just seeing doesn't require that kind of exertion.

Seeing is just seeing. Is seeing wholesome or unwholesome? It's neither! However, unwholesome mental states have many opportunities to arise without awareness+wisdom present in seeing. Meditation is about cultivating right attitude and right attention and developing *sati*, *samādhi,* and *paññā* with whatever is happening.

You need to become skillful at meditating with your eyes open if you want to take this meditation into your daily life. This means becoming skillful at practicing with and learning about any object you encounter.

The mind works in similar ways when it's looking and when it's listening. It is just working through two different sense doors. Are you aware that you are looking? The mind that is looking is looking. The mind that is listening is listening. When looking or listening, the mind has to pay attention to an object. If you know that you are looking, there is awareness already and you can recognize the mind.

There are countless instances during the day when you are looking. How many times have you noticed this throughout the day? Many defilements arise in relation to eye sense objects every time you look without awareness+wisdom. *The fires of defilements are burning.* You need to learn how to practice while looking. You need to learn how to look with awareness.

In the Satipaṭṭhāna Sutta, the Buddha gave guidance on how to speak with awareness+wisdom. We only have to consider the difficulties that have arisen out of miscommunications with each other to appreciate skillful talking. While beginning yogis are initially asked to refrain from speaking, a longer-term yogi ought to learn to talk with awareness+wisdom. We are developing this skill for our main places of practice: the home, workplace, office, or business. No one will be practicing at a meditation center her whole life but by learning how to practice for outside, both the mundane affairs and meditation for the supramundane can go hand-in-hand.

When talking, beginning with an awareness of any object is fine. With further practice, you'll become aware of what is happening in the mind as well as in the body. The mind is doing its own work of talking and you just let that happen naturally. The awareness can see how the mind is working. What is it thinking? What does the mind feel? What is it paying attention to? It's crucial to be aware of the kind of mind you are speaking with. Difficulties and suffering are a certainty in speech motivated by defilements while situations work out smoothly when there is wisdom.

So shouldn't you practice to have awareness+wisdom in speaking? Who is talking? Is there a speaker? You can recognize the speaking process as another mind and body process.

You walk back to your room from the Dhamma Hall. When do you have the intention to open the door? Some people have their keys ready in their hands on the walkway, while others have it ready by the stairs. Do you know you are going up the stairs? When you open the door, how much of the door-opening process do you know? *What are you hearing?* Can you be aware of what you are hearing if your attention is only on opening the door? That's why I say you need this expansive awareness.

Some people spend lots of energy for their sitting meditation, only to let go of everything (including awareness) when they get up. Momentum dies right then and there!

What does it mean, without a break? This is the most important part of this practice. How much are you aware of as you get up from sitting meditation?

When does the intention to get up arise? What else do you know? Are you aware of your body turning? Do you know your body turning? You move, shift, push off, get up, then what? Do you look around at other people in the Dhamma Hall?

Please work to understand the value of a mind filled with awareness and wisdom. What is the state of a mind that has this awareness+wisdom? What is the state of mind that is awake and alert? Are you able to distinguish different mental states?

A yogi reported, "I've been observing this painful sensation for over an hour now and the pain increases but my meditation does not improve. I'm going around in circles."

Right now this yogi is paying attention for an hour. If she is fully aware that she is paying attention for one hour, wouldn't this yogi have built up *sati* and *samādhi* in that time period? In this case, *lobha* looks for a specific result, i.e., for this painful sensation to go away. When things don't turn out as she had hoped or wanted, the yogi thinks that she is not progressing in meditation. Can faith and confidence increase with this way of thinking? Or will there be disappointment? This kind of wrong thinking, considered wrong attitude, wrong frame of mind, wrong attention (*ayoniso manasikāra*) is motivated by defilements in the underlying ideas.

Alternatively, if this yogi viewed this one hour as one where *sati*, *samādhi*, and *paññā* were developing, that becomes right attitude, right frame of mind and right attention (*yoniso manasikāra*). This is how confidence in oneself and faith in the practice grows.

Please consider the yogi's statement. How do we measure our progress in meditation? The development of *sati*, *samādhi*, *paññā*, and an increase in wholesome states of mind and a decrease in defilements is progress in Dhamma.

One yogi related that his sitting meditation was improving day by day and so he wanted to sit more frequently for longer periods.

Why does this yogi think this way? Actually, what should happen is that instead of wanting to sit more, the yogi should want to practice more consistently and continuously in any posture. Instead the yogi connected the "good" meditation to the sitting and so paid more attention to the posture. It's difficult to recognize the mind at work when paying more attention to the object and to what is happening.

Mistaken ideas regarding meditation come about from not being able to see the workings of the observing mind. We may not recognize that the pleasant feelings or what we may consider "good sittings" are all effects resulting from their own causes and conditions (which we failed to notice). Only the kind of wisdom that has an expansive, aerial, birds-eye-view of both mind and objects happening together and their processes is able to understand cause-and-effect relationships. Wisdom further builds up and strengthens with each new understanding that completes the picture.

Where there is a cause, there will be an effect. My teacher would always ask about the causes. He always wanted to know the causes. I would go and tell him about seeing the beginning, the middle, and end and rising and falling. Sayadawgyi would then ask, "Why did it arise?" "Why did it end?" I didn't know. (*Laughs*) I knew that there was rising and falling but I didn't know why. What was arising? So how could I believe it? He just asked simply, "Why did it happen?" No one could answer. Everyone was just looking for this arising and passing away and we were satisfied with just arising and passing away.

Buddhism in brief is about understanding cause and effect. We must know when *sati* is present and know when *sati* is absent. We need to know the causes for *sati* to happen and how *sati* can be increased. Similarly, we need to know when *samādhi* is present and to know when *samādhi* is absent. We also need to know the causes that led to the increase in *samādhi*. I will also add one more thing: We need to also know why we lose *samādhi*.

It is the same with defilements. We have to know when defilements are present, when they're absent, when they come in or intensify and when they go down in intensity. Why did they go down in intensity?

It has been some time that you've been observing this mind and body. How much more do you understand now? How deep is this understanding?

A fellow yogi observes objects. I also observe objects. Can we have the same levels of understanding of these experiences? Is it possible for someone who has just started practicing to have the same level of understanding as someone who has been practicing for a long time (in the right way)?

The practice has stalled if the current level of understanding is about the same as the previous level of understanding. Knowing and wisdom should not stand still but always be advancing. As much as knowing and understanding increase, so too does one's skill in the practice of meditation. This means the meditation is thriving.

When you see thoughts like, "Oh my meditation is not improving," please check the attitude in the mind. These thoughts can come up if you have been paying more attention to what is happening (objects) without recognizing the wanting and expectations working in the background. See:

- Is it because you haven't achieved what you expected to achieve?
- Is it because you are not getting what you wanted?
- Do you see that you are getting as much as you are practicing?

There are very few people who recognize that it is also a part of meditation when they ease up the mind that was tight or constricted.

Are you practicing in a certain place because you think it's good for meditation? Or are you practicing because you realize that this is wholesome, because you understand the value of this practice? Please first work to appreciate the goodness and value inherent in this practice.

How much more do you know about the processes and objects you've been watching for so many years now? How much do you know about objects? This understanding is important and there needs to be a curiosity, a willingness to explore, to learn, and to understand. You get to taste food at every single meal. How much more do you understand now about taste?

Reflect on these things as you practice daily. The seeing, hearing, tasting, smelling, touching, and thinking are all experiences and mind. You know when there is happiness and you know when there is sadness. How much more do you understand about these mental states now than before? In comparison, how different are the levels of defilements when the mind comes in contact with objects now?

When you reflect on Dhamma, reflect on things relevant to your experience of Dhamma. You'll need awareness to know what is happening and you'll also be more in the present moment instead of lost in thoughts.

You can't force the Dhamma to come to you. You need to be patient, but never forget the practice—that is what it means to help the Buddha's Dispensation (*sasana*).

Dhamma in the Mornings I

The following are translations of two of Ashin Tejaniya's morning Dhamma reminders given at the Shwe Oo Min Meditation Center. The talks have been edited and organized into related sections.

***

DAY 1
THE MEDITATING MIND

Keep your mind as calm and as relaxed as possible, not too tense or too lax. Don't be too anxious about your practice. The mind needs to be able to adjust accordingly, walking the middle road between too much and too little effort, neither overzealous nor disinterested. The wise mind makes adjustments as needed during meditation.

Sometimes, even with all this fine-tuning, there might still be craving (*lobha*). You may also find that you are feeling drowsy even with faith and confidence (*saddhā*) in the mind. The mind may still be weak due to defilements or there

may be a great deal of wanting and expectations in the mind. So be calm and relaxed.

---

*Rather than thinking, "I'm practicing; I'm putting in effort,"
be satisfied with knowing what is happening, "I will work just to know."*

What can you know? It's very simple. You can only know as much as the momentum that you have will allow. The mind that is meditating should be relaxed, calm, and natural. There is no need to put in too much energy or to focus in on something. Take the view that everything happening in the mind and body is happening according to nature. This is all dhamma nature at work.

CURIOSITY AND INTEREST

Have the mindset that you will not desire experiences, including not wanting something to happen. You just do what needs to be done and let whatever happens, happen. However, if there is no wholesome desire to practice, nothing happens and if there is too much wanting for something, it doesn't work either. So what should you do? What is too much and what is too little?

The mind just needs to be interested. Attentive curiosity and interest are important. You can't make anything arise or disappear through craving or aversion, so be aware of whatever is happening. Try not to forget what is happening. Remember that having expectations indicates there is some greed in the mind. Be aware of all the arising, all the passing away. Work very simply and remind yourself to be aware. If you see, just be aware that you are seeing. That is enough.

> *Let whatever happens happen.*
> *The things that are happening are just nature.*

Remind yourself that they have nothing to do with *you*. Those who understand natural laws can understand their principles. Understanding natural laws very clearly is wisdom; he who understands these laws understands nature.

Do you want to know? Please check yourself. The fact that you all came to practice means that you do want to know. You are meditating here because you wish to know the truth, to discover reality. Your key reason for being at the center is to give yourself the time to become aware of the mind and body. To see the connections and relationships between the mind and body and making a habit of seeing these connections is what you have come here to practice. The mind gets energized through this wholesome desire for learning and the wish to understand.

Keep it simple! It's good if there is knowing; it's not good if there is no knowing. There is a Burmese saying: "Ignorance is worse than being deprived." But far worse than being ignorant is not wanting to know!

WAIT AND WATCH

What is happening in the body? There are the six sense doors. Five involve the eyes, the ears, the nose, the tongue and the body. The sixth is the mind. Therefore there are six kinds of objects arising at the six sense doors. Sights are objects of knowing and sounds are objects of knowing.

> *Seeing and hearing are not happening externally.*
> *They are happening inside.*

Objects are just objects; they are neither good nor bad. Nature is just nature. An object is something that is to be known by the mind. Sound is an object. Silence is also an object. You are aware of it because its nature is to be known.

> *A thought is an object to be known just as*
> *the absence of thoughts is an object to be known.*
> *What is the difference?*

Is it good to have many thoughts? Is it bad? Is it good to have no thoughts? Is that bad? Having many thoughts or having few thoughts is neither good nor bad. Objects are just objects. If you consider them to be positive or negative, that will then be followed by likes and dislikes. That is when you get confused in your practice.

You don't need to look for or pursue objects. It's more helpful to just wait and watch. The mind sees whatever that arises. When you see, you see; when you know, you know. A yogi who practices by following objects often asks what to note next. The yogi may ask, "What else should I look for?" Alternatively, a yogi who practices by waiting and watching does not follow objects. The yogi who waits and watches uses intelligence.

Your practice needs to have the right attitude, with balanced effort, every time the mind comes in contact with objects. If the attitude is not yet right attitude, then it's necessary to work on it. How can you view objects? See that everything that is happening is all dhamma nature and that all objects follow the laws of nature.

Sights and sounds are always happening. Because the mind and object arise according to their nature, sights and sounds happen. You don't hear something because you want to hear. You don't see something because you want to see.

> *Do not think that these sensory experiences*
> *are happening because you wanted them.*
> *There is nothing happening due to your desire;*
> *everything happens due to cause and effect.*

Observe how the mind and objects interact. Are you aware only of what you want to be aware of, or of what is happening right now? Do you only observe what the mind is attracted to? Things happen according to their nature and awareness just waits and watches.

You will see things as they are if there is no greed (*lobha*), aversion (*dosa*), or delusion (*moha*) in the mind. *Lobha* is always searching for something to like. Is there really something to be desired within the object itself? Or does the *nature of liking* desire this object? *Lobha*'s nature is to like, grasp, and cling. You only *think* you like this object because of *lobha*'s nature of liking and *moha*'s nature to obscure an object's true characteristics. Delusion further confuses the mind into desiring more of the object. There's no stopping this cycle of suffering (*saṃsāra*).

There is nothing to be liked about an object. There is also nothing that you get just because you like it. You only get things when the conditions are ripe for you to get them. Whatever is happening is due to nature; you just wait and watch this process objectively. If craving is absent, you will just see what is to be seen. There is nothing attractive about what is happening. There only needs to be knowing.

LOBHA IS STICKY LIKE GLUE

> *Lobha is always present.*
> *Lobha's nature is wanting or craving*
> *and its nature is to exaggerate things.*
> *It is very sticky like glue; it doesn't let go or release.*
> *It never feels satisfied or contented because it thinks*
> *there is too little, there is never enough.*

As a yogi you can see how *lobha* comes in and creates trouble in the practice. Just try to pay attention to this. As long as you don't understand the way *lobha* works and its different tricks, you will be at its mercy. *Lobha* is craving; it always wants more. When you notice *lobha*, study it intently. How are you meditating under *lobha*'s influence? How does *lobha* think? You can't fully understand *lobha* through second-hand knowledge. Only through your very own experience of *lobha* in all of its workings, in all of its aspects will you really understand *lobha*.

To be contented is wholesome; to be discontented is *lobha*. If you are contented with the results of your practice, when you understand that you get as much as you put into the practice, then you have *samādhi*. It is *lobha* that isn't satisfied with the results of the practice. You are practicing as much as possible and you'll get that much back in return. Be contented with that. You will do as much as you can and be satisfied with what you get.

UNDERSTANDING THE NOBLE TRUTH OF DUKKHA

Vipassanā *samādhi* develops out of continuous awareness, along with right view and right attitude. *Samādhi* arises and there is peace when there is continuous awareness, with the right attitude and right view. What is unique about this? Should there be desire for a peaceful mind state? Should there be aversion to agitation? When there is a cause, there is an effect. Because there are conditions for contact, there is contact.

There is craving for comfort and happiness. There is also aversion to agitation and unhappiness. Happiness and discomfort are just feelings. The experience is only to be experienced; the object is only an object. Whether good or bad, feelings are just feelings. Wisdom recognizes this and releases the grip of *lobha* that desires good experiences.

Only when the mind does not perceive experiences as pleasing will it understand the Noble Truth of *dukkha*. As long as the mind perceives experiences as pleasing, then the Noble Truth of *dukkha* is still far from being understood.

People think that they see the truth of *dukkha* only when they experience suffering. If that is so, how can they understand that experiencing calm (*samādhi*), the moments of bliss or delight (*pīti*), or of tranquility (*passaddhi*), are also *dukkha*? So long as *moha* is present and considers any of these experiences as pleasing, the Noble Truth of *dukkha* can't be understood yet. Because people listen with defilements when they hear about the Noble Truth of *dukkha*, they think it is about experiencing bodily or mental suffering. In fact, that is *dosa* at work.

Whatever is happening is *dukkha*. Don't look at what is happening with aversion or you will become depressed. The Noble Truth of *dukkha* is discerned by the wise mind and is totally opposite to the kind of *dukkha* one *feels*. The understanding of the truth of *dukkha* is wisdom. The mind feels strength, energy, freedom, and detachment with this understanding. The mind is devoid of craving and defilements. Whereas the experience of *dukkha* is exhausting, the true realization of *dukkha* is free from attachment and free of defilements.

WISDOM HAS NO PREFERENCE

As you continue to practice, observe when awareness is present and when awareness is absent, when wisdom is present and when wisdom is absent. Wisdom naturally understands what is beneficial and what is not beneficial. You are practicing to learn to watch the mind and body. Insights will grow according to your understanding and what you can know. What is more beneficial: To have awareness or to lack awareness, to develop wisdom or not develop wisdom? You can investigate and analyze this for yourself.

However much we plead for a blind person to see, he will not be able to see. Likewise, no matter how often we ask a person to see ultimate reality (*paramattha*), he will not understand its principles when there is no wisdom. Only the wise, discerning mind can understand the nature of *paramattha*.

---

*Wisdom has no preference
to see one thing over another.*

Without the desire to see specific things, all you have to do is keep your eyes open and you can be aware. It is obvious; you know that you are seeing. The desire to see specific things or experiences stems from *lobha*. Wisdom can't arise when the mind is filled with *lobha*. When you observe with *lobha*, only more *lobha* will arise. However, it is wisdom that recognizes when *lobha* has arisen in the mind.

Vipassanā wisdom can't be comprehended simply through intellectual thinking. The ordinary mind can't bring about insight through intellectual thinking. *Vipassanā* insight is not something that can be conceptualized through images; it is a wholly new understanding and insight of principles or nature.

It is *kusala* if wholesome states of mind are continuously followed by wholesome states of mind. *Samādhi* doesn't develop if wholesome states are

Without the desire to see specific things, all you have to do is keep your eyes open and you can be aware.

followed by unwholesome states. There is *samādhi* when the previous mind is wholesome, if the present mind is wholesome, if this is followed by wholesome mental states, and there is continuity in awareness. The absence of *sati*, *samādhi*, and *paññā* is what gives defilements opportunities to arise.

Whatever kind of work that involves defilements
will one day grow old and dull.
On the contrary, the work of knowing is never dull.

Knowing with wisdom, knowing reality, does not have the characteristic of becoming uninteresting or monotonous. It is always new and fresh. You don't get tired of knowing, as knowing is never finished. It never gets boring. You need to be happy with the work you are doing, to have interest in it. This work is for life.

When the mind sees again what is already familiar, the knowledge only becomes clearer. Wisdom deepens and you become more attentive and energized. Your understanding and field of comprehension expand. There is no end to knowing, as it is never complete. There should be no such thing as "I know," because it is never enough. You start to see things from multiple angles: You see two sides, mundane world and ultimate reality, mind and object, cause and effect.

THIS PRACTICE IS FOR ALWAYS

Remember that practice is not done only through sitting. It is not only when you sit to meditate that there is awareness. The awareness must be present at all times, in all activities. Once you have a right attitude of balanced effort without expectations, try to be continuously aware. Only then will momentum develop. It is important to learn to be aware for longer and longer periods so that you can use this momentum outside.

You are not exerting so much energy or yearning for something.
Neither the mind nor the body should become tired.
There's no need to focus.
Work with balance, calm, and continuity.

The most important aspect of meditation is the meditating mind; awareness must always be present. Observe whether the mind is working or not. Keep checking the mind to see whether awareness is present. What is the mind aware of?

It is important to practice with care, respect, and interest and practice as much as you can. You've come this far and you will get as much as you put in. Be satisfied with the *sati* and *samādhi* that develop. Finally, remember to practice consistently throughout the day, all the time, with a balanced mind and right effort.

DAY 2

The meditating mind must be a Dhamma mind. Be calm, comfortable and relaxed, with peace, faith, and intelligence. That is how you should be practicing.

Wisdom is there when there is right awareness. However, if the awareness is too focused, there's no chance for wisdom to come in. That is why we don't force, focus, control, or restrict. We don't try to make anything disappear. We are just aware of all that is happening and all that is passing away. There are no expectations or discontentment.

Do not forget. Be aware. Keeping that in mind, you have to keep checking the mind. What is the mind doing? Is it aware? *Does* it know? *What* does it know? *How much* can it know? There needs to be an alertness to knowing objects. This means knowing when hearing happens, when contact happens. The mind is alert when the mind knows objects as contact happens.

There is the Dhamma we must *have* and there is the dhamma we must *know*. When we refer to the Dhamma we must *have*, we mean the five spiritual faculties of *sati*, *samādhi*, *viriya*, *saddhā*, and *paññā*. The dhamma we must *know* is what is happening in the mind and body. Meditation is the practice of cultivating and developing the Dhamma that we don't already have, to come to know what we don't already know.

CULTIVATING WHOLESOME QUALITIES

We meditate to develop the *sati*, *samādhi*, *viriya*, *saddhā*, and *paññā* that are not yet present in the mind. The stronger these five spiritual faculties become, the weaker the defilements become.

When sati is present, defilements become weak.
When samādhi is present, defilements become weak.
When viriya is present, defilements become weak.
When saddhā is present, defilements become weak.
When paññā is present, defilements become weak.

What is important is that we meditate to nurture and cultivate these currently weak, wholesome mental qualities so that they can grow stronger and stronger. Mindfulness meditation is not about seeking unique experiences. Wisdom does not have the desire for specific things to happen.

Saddhā and *viriya* have the wish to keep up the practice. *Viriya* is the wish to practice continuously and with perseverance. *Saddhā* wants to continue meditation because it knows the value of the practice. Merely focusing on results is the work of *lobha*. If you are pleased that you see the object you wanted to see, that is the work of *lobha*. Dissatisfaction with getting an object other than what you want to see is *dosa*. These are both defilements!

ALL OBJECTS ARE DHAMMA NATURE

All objects are dhamma nature, dhamma phenomena. You can't hold onto any object with *lobha*. Don't perceive any objects or experiences as good or bad as no object or experience is better than any other experience or object. Objects are just objects. They are to be known. That is all.

Don't go looking for objects or experiences that you may *think* are good. The search for good experiences is coming at the bidding of *lobha*. You are not meditating to get good experiences. If there's thinking right now or you are feeling heat, just know what is happening. What are they? All are just phenomena or objects.

The work of meditation is not to develop objects
which are just happening through their own causes;
the work of meditation is to cultivate the five spiritual faculties
of sati, samādhi, viriya, saddhā, and paññā.

ENJOYING THE PRACTICE

Is it better to delight in a "good sitting" or better to have awareness? It is not about liking the results but about enjoying the practice itself. You will continue to practice on your own when you are interested in and happy

Objects are just objects. They are to be known.

to practice and when you are invigorated by the work you are doing. Only when you see and understand the effects of your practice will you want to pay attention to becoming skillful in fulfilling the causes and conditions. If the causes are good, the effects will also be good. Let whatever is happening, happen but don't forget the knowing. Investigate and learn.

TASTE OF DHAMMA

Naturally, if there are wholesome mental states, there will be peace. It is important that the meditating mind is a wholesome mind or working towards wholesomeness. *Sati, samādhi, viriya, saddhā,* and *paññā* are all wholesome. Out of all the wholesome actions we can do (*dāna, sīla, samādhi,* and *paññā*), cultivating wholesome mental qualities through *vipassanā bhāvanā* (*paññā*) is the highest one.

Most people in this world like to enjoy the taste of good feelings or sensations.

It is said that among all tastes, the best taste is the taste of Dhamma.
The taste of Dhamma is not just a feeling of peace—
it is the supreme taste of knowing and understanding.

You need to taste the full flavors of Dhamma: Of knowing, of awareness, and of understanding.

Dhamma in the Mornings II

The following are transcribed selections of Ashin Tejaniya's English morning Dhamma reminders recorded over a six-month period from October 2009 to March 2010. We've tried to keep Ashin Tejaniya's rhythm and style of speaking intact while organizing the morning reminders into discrete themes and eliminating some repetition in the text.

***

MINDFULNESS MEDITATION IS A LEARNING PROCESS

Meditation is about cultivating the good qualities of mind. We are just trying to cultivate moment-to-moment, very simple. Don't forget what is happening in you. If awareness is present, wisdom is also present and the mind is free, liberated. It is free from the wrong view and free from suffering.

Mindfulness meditation is a learning process, not a creative process. So, we are not trying to do anything. We just wait and watch what is happening as it is, not wanting, no expectations. We just practice simply and continuously.

We are not trying to make something happen, to resist anything, or to make anything disappear. We are not trying to create something. We are in the present moment, just staying in the present moment by being awake, knowing, and aware.

CHECKING THE ATTITUDE

We check our attitude first before we meditate. What attitude, what background ideas do you have when you meditate?

> *Do you want anything?*
> *Do you expect anything?*
> *Why are you meditating?*
> *Why are you being mindful?*

We want to understand—that is why we are watching and learning. We are not trying to control anything. We are not trying to create anything. We simply want to be in the present moment: Awake, alert, aware.

Check your state of mind. Check your quality of awareness in the observing mind. Is it tense or relaxed? What attitude do you have? Is the attitude right or wrong? Very often you need to check your attitude. When you are checking your mind, awareness is already present. Only reminding and checking is enough. Just check your effort, energy and quality of mind. How do you feel when you are mindful?

Wait and watch, very simply, with the right attitude. You don't want to control the experience. You don't want to change the object or experience. Whatever is happening is not your responsibility. Your responsibility is right attitude and checking if awareness is present or not and that it is moment-to-moment. Check, learn, and have interest.

INTEREST IN THE ACTIVITY OF THE MIND

If the mind doesn't want anything, it is peaceful and relaxed. Think about it as it is. Try to have interest in the activity of the mind. The mind knows, the mind is paying attention and the mind feels.

The object is not very important. Don't go looking for it. Take care of the quality of your mind. Check the quality of your mind—what attitude, what idea, and what states of mind are there when you meditate? Take care of your awareness and maintain your awareness. Don't attach to anything. Don't resist anything.

So, how do you do this? If you don't have the right attitude or the right idea, the mind will always attach to something or resist something. The mind never rests. If you don't have wisdom you can't go the middle-way. When you use wisdom, right attitude, right idea, and right thought, the mind follows the middle-way. With equanimity and understanding nature as it is there is no problem. At that time you can learn more deeply.

Don't forget to think the right way, have the right information, right idea, and right attitude. What are you doing now? What is the mind doing? What is happening in the mind? Whatever is happening, everything is okay, no problem. Let it be. Stay with the awareness. In the present moment we are trying to be awake, alert, and interested. We are not trying to go anywhere. We are not trying to get anything. We only need to have right view, awareness, and interest.

---

*Experience is happening and
objects are happening all the time.
Whatever is happening is not our responsibility—
it is as it is.*

Our responsibility is to think the right way, to have the right attitude, and to be aware continuously. Right thought is very important; right attitude, right thought means perceiving everything as nature. Object is object. Everything is nature. Nothing is a problem. We want to know and we want to understand nature as it is.

Check your energy: How much energy do you use? If you use too much energy, the mind becomes tense. Are you sure awareness is present? If you can see

What is the mind doing?
What is happening in the mind?

awareness, awareness is surely present. We are not trying to get something. Meditation is cultivation of awareness moment-to-moment. We don't use too much energy, focusing, penetration, or concentration. Just remember in the present moment. If you don't want anything, the mind is very peaceful.

You can't get anything because you want it. Whatever you get is because of conditions. Because the cause is fulfilled, the effect comes. Not because you want it to. You need to pay attention to awareness, to the meditating mind. In the present moment, is awareness present or not? Don't follow the object. The object is not very important. The mind is more important. You need to check what state of mind, what attitude you have when you meditate. Check your energy: How much energy do you use? Is the mind relaxed or not, tense or not? You don't need too much effort to know the object. The mind naturally can know the object. Your responsibility is to take care of your awareness. Is it present or not?

We are not trying to go anywhere. We don't expect anything. We are not trying to create anything. We are being aware present moment by present moment. The meditating mind must be simple. We are waiting. We wait and watch, as it is, thinking about nature as nature. Nature is not ours, not others', no body. Nature is no person, nobody. It's all a natural process as there are causes and there are effects. The cause and effect process and conditioning are nature. The mind is aware, the mind is feeling, the mind is paying attention, and the mind is recognizing. Everything is mind. Mind is working. Mind is happening. Nature is happening, nature is working.

Why are you aware? Don't forget what you are doing, don't forget why you are doing this. What is the state of your observing mind? You are cultivating awareness and watching continuously. This is moment-to-moment cultivation. The meditating mind must have the right attitude. The practice must be done the right way. Experience is always happening. What [background] idea do you have in your practice? What state of mind are you watching it with? What point of view are you looking at it with? When you are not expecting anything, when you don't want anything, at that time, understanding can arise.

UNDERSTANDING OBJECTS AS OBJECTS

> *Any object or experience that appears*
> *should not disturb your practice.*
> *Objects are helping your awareness.*
> *You can use any object to grow*
> *sīla, samādhi, and paññā.*

If you have right attitude then everything is no problem and the object does not disturb you. Any object is a dhamma object, dhamma nature. Even pain can be an object. Pain is an object; no pain is also an object. Object is object; if you understand object as object, the mind can't attach and can't resist. The mind with no craving and no aversion has *samādhi*.

Now, the sound of this machine is obvious [the microphone is creating feedback]. Is this sound a problem? Think about it as it is. Dhamma nature is arising, appearing. It becomes an object that the mind can then know. You can be aware of this object and you can cultivate this awareness, concentration, and wisdom. Use this object. If you have the right attitude, you can cultivate awareness, concentration, and wisdom.

The object helps you to be aware, awake, and alert.
Because of the object you can learn,
you can be aware, and you can understand.

In the present moment we just try to be awake and alert. With no expectation, or greed, the mind is very peaceful and free. In the present moment we need to be alert, awake, and ready. We are just trying moment-to-moment to be awake. Because of wanting, because of desire, we are not free. If we want something, if we are resistant, the mind is not awake. Without expectation, without resisting, the mind is awakened. Awakening means we know and understand what is happening. With everything, any experience in the present moment, there is only mind, objects, and awareness. We need to have the right attitude in the awareness. Nature is nature, feeling is just feeling.

ARE YOU SURE AWARENESS IS THERE?

The meaning of awareness is not forgetting. This means not forgetting to think the right way, not forgetting to be aware, not forgetting the right object. Awareness is not forgetting. Remembering and reminding is awareness.

Are you sure awareness is present? Recognize when awareness is present. If awareness is present then the object is already there. You don't need to focus on the object. You just need to check if awareness is present or not, whether awareness is continuous or not. Whatever is happening in the mind and body is not your responsibility. Experience is experience. The experience is not your responsibility.

Your responsibility is to have the right attitude
and to be aware continuously.
Check again and again, whether you have
the right or wrong attitude.
Reminding, checking, remembering—this is enough.
You don't need to use too much energy to focus.

How does the mind feel when it is aware? Relaxed or not, tense or not? Check your mental state. The meditation mind must be relaxed, peaceful, and interested. When you are meditating, whatever is happening, no experience should disturb you. Everything is nature, dhamma, or object. Whatever is happening is for learning. You are not looking for any object. You are checking your quality of mind, the quality of the watching mind. Do you have the right attitude or not? Is the mind relaxed or not?

Check your quality of mind, the quality of awareness, how the mind is working, if the meditating mind is interested, if awareness is present. You are checking, reminding, and remembering moment-to-moment. If the mind is stronger and stronger, the watching mind stronger and stronger, it is doing its job. Your responsibility is only to maintain awareness, moment-to-moment *in a relaxed way* and with interest.

DON'T FOLLOW THE OBJECT

You need to take care of awareness, not objects. If you are aware, some object is already there. You are cultivating awareness continuously. You don't do anything with the object. Stay with the awareness. It is more important that you take care of your awareness, checking and continuing like this, moment-to-moment. So simple! Whatever objects the mind is knowing, let it be. The mind knows some object, the mind knows this object or that object. You are waiting and watching how the mind is working. Where is the mind? The mind is knowing, so continue to try to be knowing continuously. Sometimes you can get stuck on one object. You can know any object and you can know anything about an object. If the mind slowly calms down and just checks, the mind can know anything.

How does the mind react to any experience?
Is the mind aware or not?
When you notice an object, how do you feel?
What do you think?

Being continuously aware is very important. If you want continuous awareness, you must see, you must know that awareness is present or not. If you follow the object, awareness can't be continuous. If you check that awareness is present, the object is already there. There is no need to follow the object, no need to focus on the object. It's a waste of time and energy and not necessary. If you notice your awareness is present the object is already happening. You don't want to fixate on one object. With any object, you just want to know that nature is happening.

The meditating mind is important. Knowing, being aware, the mind is working, the mind is aware, the mind is watching. You must have right attitude and right idea. Whatever is happening is experience. The meaning is not important. Just recognizing the experience is okay. You are aware of what is happening. Hearing is happening. You are not trying to *think about* the meaning, you are trying to be aware of the experience. Knowing you are hearing is enough. Before you are hearing, before you are listening, awareness must be ready. If awareness is continuous, awareness is always waiting and watching. Now you are hearing the sound and silence, not only the sound, but the silence also. Object is the experience, experience is the object.

We are not following any object. We let the object come. The object is already there and the experience is always there. We are not trying to follow the object, focus on the object. Why are we aware? Why are we watching? We must have the right idea, right motivation, and right knowledge. We want to understand and know the real nature of experience. We want to understand. That's why we are learning and that's why we are watching.

VIPASSANĀ SAMĀDHI

Samādhi comes from right attitude, right idea, and right knowledge. You are not trying to do anything with craving. You are not trying to do anything with aversion or delusion. You are aware in the present moment with the right attitude. Whatever is happening in the mind and body is just nature. If you think this way that nature is nature, feeling is feeling, the mind is not reacting, liking or disliking. So the mind is peaceful and stable.

Whatever is happening is not your responsibility. Your responsibility is to try to think the right way and to try to be aware continuously. Right view and right thought is very important. With right view and right thought, *samādhi* is already there. Check in your mind: If there is no craving, no aversion, and no reaction, this is also *samādhi*. This is *vipassanā samādhi* and *sammā-samādhi*. Because of understanding, because of right view, because of right thought, the mind is already calm, peaceful and stable.

The meaning of *samādhi* is stability of mind, not focusing. Just ask yourself how the mind is working, why the mind is working and if the mind is relaxed. Check the quality of mind. With just checking, you don't need too much energy to be mindful. If you have the right view, right idea, and right thought then the mind is stable. When the mind is calm and peaceful, this is *samādhi*. If there is no *lobha*, this is *samādhi*. If there is no *dosa*, this is also *samādhi*. This is *vipassanā samādhi*.

EXPECTATIONS AND PATIENCE

For any experience that appears, check to see whether you have a reaction. Are you interested in being mindful? Are you interested in practicing? Why are you aware? Your practice should be simple and natural, with no expectation. You are not trying to gain something. You are trying to be aware in the present moment. If your expectations are high, the mind will not have any interest. It can't be satisfied with what it already has. The mind becomes bored or disinterested.

> *If you understand in the present moment*
> *what you are doing and already getting,*
> *understand clearly, the mind can be satisfied or interested.*
> *Meditation is a learning process. You can't hurry.*

Meditation is recognizing what is happening. Sometimes expectations arise but it's not a problem. The only thing you need to do is to recognize that the expectation is there. Don't judge this expectation. Meditation is not about trying to change anything or trying to control anything. It is just recognizing what is happening. Don't complicate things in the present moment. Be simple and just know. If you don't have expectations (not wanting anything) the mind is already at peace.

BEING PRESENT

Stay with the peace in the present moment. Just be in the present moment, stay in the present moment. The present moment is the only thing that exists. Past does not exist and future does not exist either. *Now*, stay in the present moment, peacefully. Just simply be aware in the present moment; the mind is very peaceful not wanting anything. If wanting or craving exists, your duty is just to recognize. No need to judge what is happening.

> *When we meditate, there is no need to hurry.*
> *We are not going anywhere.*
> *We are staying in the present moment fully.*

If you can stay in the present moment you can be satisfied. Because of knowing, you understand what is happening now, understand what is going on in the present moment, this is real life. Whatever you put into the practice you get in return. If you don't know what you are already getting, you will want more. You get as much as you put in. If you can stay fully in the present moment, expectations won't come. No need to regret the past. No need to expect the future. You are trying to think the right way. Thinking is very powerful. If your thinking is reasonable, if your thinking is right, the mind is already calm, relaxed and peaceful.

WHEN THE MIND IS INTERESTED, WISDOM IS WORKING

Because of knowledge, because of wisdom, the mind is peaceful and stable already. So that's why there's no need to use too much focusing. Check the mind, what the mind is thinking and what the mind is knowing. Only interest is necessary. When the mind is interested, wisdom is working.

When we are meditating and the mind thinks about the Dhamma, about practice, nature, or object, this thinking makes our awareness stronger and stronger, because of interest. The dhamma nature is more awake and alert because of checking. If our minds are thinking [these right thoughts] the mind can't be sleepy. Then we are thinking the right way. We must both **think** about the practice **and practice**. We are not blindly aware. Awareness alone is not enough. Awareness and wisdom come together. If someone is aware continuously, naturally wisdom will slowly, slowly grow.

> *Defilements do their job and wisdom also does its job.*
> *We already have intelligence. We use our knowledge,*
> *intelligence and effort to practice.*

When we don't have craving, aversion, worry or anxiety in the present moment, the mind is free and peaceful because of knowledge, wisdom and awareness. Do you understand this? *It's not only about being mindful. We are being aware, thinking, and recognizing.*

We should be thinking about the practice. If we are thinking the right way, the mind can't think the wrong way. We prevent delusion when we are aware and when we understand. Knowing what is happening is also right view. Whether it is good or bad, we know what is happening in the present moment.

So, don't forget why you are doing this; don't forget why, for what, with what motivation. Do you want to get something? Are you sure awareness is present? If it is present, what do you understand? Sometimes you need to use the questions of what, why, and how. But the answer is not important. Interest is important. You only need interest. You can't and you don't want to get results immediately.

THE BENEFITS OF AWARENESS

When you are aware continuously, how do you feel? In the present moment, *now*, do you want anything? Do you have expectations? What are you doing? If awareness is present in this moment, how do you feel? If awareness is lost, what is different? Having awareness and not having awareness: How is the mind different?

Do you understand the value of awareness? Stay with the awareness. *All objects come to awareness.* What is the difference between having awareness and not having awareness? There is a different quality of mind. You need to understand the value of awareness. If you are aware, how do you feel? When you are meditating, is the mind tense or not, relaxed or not? When you are interested, wisdom is working. Because of the object, you can be aware.

Continuity is very important, moment-to-moment and moment by moment. And momentum, momentum is nature, nature is dhamma. Continuity of practice becomes a habit; habit becomes nature. Habit becomes nature when the practice gains momentum and the dhamma is working, nature is working, "nobody" is meditating, and nobody is practicing. Nature is practice. Momentum comes because of the cause and effect process.

Any time awareness is present, the mind is safe,
secure, meaningful and alive.
If we're not aware, we are lost, and we've lost meaning.

We don't know what's happening in the present moment. We are blind and we are deaf. Awareness and lack of awareness have two very different qualities. If we have awareness with wisdom (depending on the wisdom quality) awareness will be stronger. The value is also very different.

We need to understand that as much as we put into practice we get in return. If we don't understand what we already have, we can't be satisfied. If we have too many expectations, we don't know what we have. If our expectations are too high, we can't be satisfied with what we already have.

We need to appreciate what we are doing. We should understand the value of what we are doing. What is the benefit of doing this? What is the result if we don't do this? If we are not doing this, what is happening? We are cultivating and growing these good qualities of mind, moment-to-moment.

ON RIGHT EFFORT AND ENERGY

Check your energy and how much energy you use. You don't need too much energy to know something, to be aware. If there's an expectation or if you want something, the mind uses more energy. Check your state of mind. Don't let the mind be tense or tired. The meditating mind must be relaxed. Don't use too much energy to be focused.

We don't need to use too much energy to know the object. Naturally the mind can know the object. We need to continually remind ourselves and recognize the importance of staying in the present moment, moment by moment.

We don't need to use too much effort or too much energy to be focused, to be mindful. The nature of the mind can know the object naturally, so we don't need to try to know the object. If the mind is relaxed, the mind knows something about itself. The meaning of effort is to try to continue, try to be patient, try to be relaxed. Effort is doing what we should do and not doing what should not be done. Effort is also to try to reduce defilements. Making awareness continuous is also effort.

ON RIGHT PRACTICE

Sometimes we sit and stop meditating; to stop meditating is wrong meditation. Wrong attitude and wrong meditation is "stopping," meaning right meditation is "starting". The mind can know, the mind has momentum already, awareness all the time, it knows many things. If you have right idea, right attitude, right thinking, the mind immediately calms down, becomes peaceful. We stop the wrong practice, meaning we start the right practice.

THE NOBLE EIGHTFOLD PATH

We are practicing the Noble Eightfold Path. In this moment we can hear. The fact that we are aware that we are hearing is right view. We know what is happening in the present moment. This is right view. This is nature. This is experience. Object is object. Experience is experience. There's no body, no person. If we have this attitude and we are aware of what is happening, this is right view and right thought.

> *When we have right view and right thought,*
> *we can't speak wrongly, we can't act wrongly,*
> *and we can't live wrongly.*
> *This is right speech, right action, and right livelihood.*

Being aware is right action. Then we have right effort, right awareness, and right *samādhi*. This is the Noble Eightfold Path.

FIVE SPIRITUAL FACULTIES (INDRIYA)

Right effort is perseverance. Effort means being persistent, being patient, continuing again and again, and not giving up. This is the meaning of effort. Don't use too much energy. Check your quality of *sati*, *samādhi*, *viriya*, *saddhā*, and *paññā*. How much interest do you have? Are you willing to practice? *Paññā* is understanding, wisdom. So you need to check if awareness is present in the mind. Is understanding present? Is wisdom present? Check the quality of the watching, meditating mind. The mind is meditating. The mind is watching. The mind is practicing.

You don't use too much energy to practice. You are just watching with the right attitude, right idea, and interest. You need to know if awareness is present or not. You need to appreciate that awareness is present, which you are recognizing, being aware of what is going on.

> *You should know if samādhi is present or not.*
> *Is samādhi present?*
> *If you know there's no samādhi,*
> *you know there's no samādhi.*

Because you are aware, you know. If you recognize clearly whether awareness is present or not, if you recognize clearly that samādhi is present or not, wisdom is present or not, if you recognize clearly that wisdom is NOT present, this in itself is wisdom! This is also understanding.

CRAVING

Craving is very tricky; it's always pushing you. Whatever you think, whatever you say, whatever you do, craving is pushing you, motivating you. There are many ways for craving to come in or arise in your mind. What do you want? Sometimes you should ask yourself: What do I want? Do I want something? There's always wanting. Because of this wanting, desire, craving, expectation (same meaning), the mind is suffering, tense, and dissatisfied.

> *If the mind doesn't want anything, it is very free.*

You can't get what you want. If you understand the principle that you can't get something because you want it and that you only get what comes from conditions, cause and effect, then desire gets weaker and weaker. Craving will be less and less. Everything happens because of cause and effect, not because you want it to happen.

My teacher once said, "If you want, it will happen. If you don't want, it will not happen." What is the meaning behind this? "If you want, it will happen" means if you want because of craving, you will suffer. The first sentence means wanting comes from craving. For example, someone doesn't like pain. He wants the pain to go away. He wants no pain. The second sentence, "If you don't want" means if you don't want through craving or aversion, then suffering doesn't happen. First "wanting" is because of craving. Second "don't want" is because of wisdom. First is origin of suffering (*samudaya*) and *dukkha*. Second is because of path knowledge (*magga ñāṇa*) and no suffering (*nirodha*). If you have craving or wanting, *lobha*, then *dosa* and aversion come. Craving and aversion are *lobha* and *dosa*. But, *magga ñāṇa*, "don't want," is because of understanding that you don't want craving and aversion. That's why suffering doesn't arise. If you want something with craving, suffering will surely arise.

You don't get something just because you wanted it. Whatever you get is because of conditioning, because of cause and effect. But people think they'll get what they want. Actually, you can only get suffering if you want something with craving.

> *If you understand that everything happens*
> *through cause and effect—*
> *everything happens because of conditions—*
> *then you won't want craving or aversion, good or bad.*
> *Suffering doesn't arise.*
> *Peace, liberation, freedom comes*
> *because you don't want anything.*

Raga khayo Nibbāna, meaning if you don't have craving, this is *Nibbāna*. If craving disappears, this is liberation. We are suffering because we don't know and we want; because we don't know, *lobha* and *dosa* exist.

ACCEPTANCE

We are trying to think the right way; we are trying to be aware. We are not complaining about what is happening. We check our quality of awareness. Reminding, checking, recognizing. Acceptance is very important. If we don't have right view or if we don't have right thought, we can't accept. If we can't accept, we can't learn. We let it be. We are not trying to change the experience. We don't change the process. We are trying to be aware.

We don't complain about what is happening. Everything is experience. Whatever is happening is happening through cause and effect. They do their job, we do our job. What should we do? We just recognize what is happening. Everything is nature.

APPRECIATE THAT THE MIND IS WORKING

We don't appreciate what we are doing. We are always complaining or thinking about what is happening. Experience may be good or bad, right or wrong—it's not important. Experience is experience. We need to appreciate and we need to recognize that the mind is working, being aware and watching. If our experience is good, the mind becomes happy. Happy, happy! If our experience is bad, we become very sad, upset. This means that we don't understand. We must understand that nature is nature and object is object. We let go of experience. We are not trying to hold onto any experience or object. We are trying to appreciate that the mind is working. We need only to check the quality of awareness of the watching, meditating mind. Is the meditating mind working or not? Is the mind interested or not? Is it strong or not? Just check.

STRENGTHENING THE MIND

Your watching mind must be strong and purified, with less defilement. If your mind is ready, understanding arises. So take care of your mind, take care of your practice and take care of your watching mind. Cultivate it so that it is stronger and stronger.

> *Depending on your quality of mind, the object may be perceived differently and the view changes.*

Our duty is to make the quality of awareness stronger. Stronger awareness means awareness and wisdom are working together continuously. This is awareness with the right view, right attitude, right idea, and right thought. If this is continuous, then the mind is stronger and stronger. We only need to do this. If the mind becomes stronger it can do its job. Dhamma does its job and nature does its job.

We are not trying to see the object. We are not trying to look for something. We are trying to make the meditating mind stronger and stronger.

How do we make the mind stronger? When we are aware, with the right attitude and right understanding, then the mind has wisdom and it becomes stronger. This is not because we are putting in a lot of energy; if we use too much energy the mind will become tired. If we try to see something, the mind

becomes tenser. We are cultivating the quality of awareness to make the mind stronger and stronger. If we have awareness with wisdom and continuity, then the mind becomes stronger and stronger. When the mind becomes stronger it can do its job.

> *For someone who has been meditating*
> *or practicing for a long time,*
> *the mind must be of a better and better quality.*
> *The mind is more aware,*
> *more stable and more peaceful.*

There is more understanding. It should be like this. When we have more understanding, we have less resistance and fewer reactions. Because of reactions, we suffer. Because of learning, we understand. With understanding comes confidence.

ANICCA, DUKKHA, ANATTA

Nothing stays the same. Everything is always changing. Nature is happening because of conditioning. Because of conditions, objects are arising. This is the meaning of *anicca*. You need to understand whatever is happening (thinking is happening, sensation is happening, knowing mind is happening, awareness is happening); you need to notice that it's happening. Arising, happening, becoming. Happening, becoming, and arising. Happening is *anicca*, happening is *dukkha,* and happening is *anatta.* When your mind is purified you can understand. You can understand happening is impermanence, happening is *dukkha*, and happening is cause and effect, *anatta*, no body. Awareness is noticing everything that is happening; object is also happening, knowing is also happening, sensation is also happening, thinking is also happening. It's all new, new, new.

SIMPLE EXPERIENCE, DEEP UNDERSTANDING

When you are aware of some sensation or some object, what do you understand about this object? *Now*, what do you understand? Do you understand something? Sometimes you can know but you don't understand. You know many objects and you are aware of many things. What is your purpose?

Defilements cover the mind. We can't understand the nature of defilement. That's why we need to understand the nature of craving, the nature of aversion, the nature of delusion. Then they have no chance to come in. When the mind is clear, without craving, without aversion, without delusion, the mind is ready to understand. When the mind is clear then wisdom can arise.

> *The experience may be very simple,*
> *but our understanding may be very deep.*
> *Because of understanding of object as object*
> *(understanding very deeply)*
> *we don't have delusion, craving, or aversion.*

We have many experiences throughout the day; we are always meeting experiences. But when our watching mind is purified, when awareness and understanding are complete, this simple experience becomes very strange [extraordinary]. Because we have always had the wrong view when knowing experience and now we have right view, right understanding, our view is opposite—very strange [extraordinary].

THE CHANCE TO PRACTICE MINDFULNESS MEDITATION IS VERY RARE

To be aware of something sounds simple, but this technique is very difficult to practice. We can practice this way, with this technique when a Buddha arises. But if we have no Buddha, we can't practice. Truly practicing mindfulness meditation is very rare.

DHAMMA IS EVERYWHERE

Because the mind is covered by defilements, we are unable to see dhamma or to understand nature as it is. What is the meaning of nature? It is cause and it is also effect. The cause and effect process itself is nature. Whatever is happening in the present moment is nature, dhamma. Even defilements become dhamma, become nature. Nature is becoming, nature is arising, knowing is arising and awareness is arising—object and mind, object and mind. In nature, there is nobody there. Nature is not *us*, not *them*, not *others*; nature is nature.

Dhamma is ever present and there is dhamma talk everywhere. Nature is also teaching us dhamma but we are unable to hear. We can't know or see dhamma because of the defilements in the mind and because there isn't enough understanding or wisdom. If we can think and see nature as it really is, the mind is *free* and free from defilements.

Dhamma is everywhere.
Dhamma is there all the time, everywhere.
Is the mind ready to understand?

Dhamma is ever present and there is dhamma talk everywhere.

If we can think and see nature as it really is,
the mind is *free* and free from defilements.

Glossary of Selected Pāli Terms

Ashin Tejaniya frequently uses key Pāli terms in Dhamma discussions and discourses. Below you will find some of the frequently used terms. This glossary is far from comprehensive, but the explanations given should be sufficient for our purposes. Please consult Buddhist texts and dictionaries for more complete definitions.

adhiṭṭhāna	determination, resolution
adosa	hatelessness
akusala (also see *kusala*)	kammically unwholesome, unskillful, unprofitable
anatta (also see *atta*)	a) not-self, non-ego, impersonality, there is no abiding substance (or an ego, a self, or a soul), there is no self-existing entity
	b) nothing can arise on its own or from a single cause and nothing can exist or move on its own
	c) one of the three universal characteristics of existence (see dukkha and anicca), understanding anatta is a liberating insight (paññā)

anicca	a) impermanence, all conditioned phenomena are impermanent, everything that comes into existence changes and passes away
	b) one of the three universal characteristics of existence (see dukkha and anatta), understanding anicca is a liberating insight (paññā)
anusaya	potential or latent defilements
appamāda	heedfulness, non-laxity, diligence, presence of self-awareness (literally: non-forgetfulness)
asammoha-sampajañña	clear knowledge of non-delusion; understanding anicca, dukkha, and anatta
atta	self, ego, personality
avijjā	synonym for moha
ayoniso manasikāra	a) wrong attitude, wrong frame of mind, wrong attention
	b) unwise consideration
	(opposite of *yoniso manasikāra*)
bhāvanā	mental development, meditation
bhāvanāmayā paññā	wisdom or knowledge acquired through direct experience, through mental development
bhava-taṇhā	craving for existence
bhikkhu	fully ordained monk, member of the Saṅgha

bojjhaṅga	the seven factors of enlightenment, also referred to as sambojjhaṅga
cetasika	mental factor (This refers to the 52 mental factors listed in the abhidhamma. Some are kammically neutral, some kammically wholesome and some kammically unwholesome.)
chanda	wholesome intention, aspiration, zeal, wholesome desire
cintāmayā paññā	wisdom or knowledge acquired by thinking and reasoning, by intellectual analysis
citta	mind
cittānupassanā	contemplation of the mind
dāna	giving, offering, generosity
dhamma	conditioned object, thing, phenomena, "natural law," "nature"
Dhamma	Teachings of the Buddha, practice of meditation
dhammānupassanā	contemplation of dhamma
dhamma-vicaya	investigation of phenomena, investigation of dhamma
diṭṭhi	view, belief, speculative opinion
	micchā-diṭṭhi (wrong view) / sammā-diṭṭhi (right view)
domanassa	any kind of unpleasant mental feeling, mentally painful feeling

Glossary of Selected Pāli Terms | 235

dosa	hatred, anger, any kind of aversion or disliking (including sadness, fear, resistance, etc.)
dukkha	a) unsatisfactoriness, pain, suffering
	b) the suffering in change
	c) the unsatisfactory nature of all existence, of all conditioned phenomena
	d) one of the three universal characteristics of existence (see anicca and anatta), understanding dukkha is a liberating insight (paññā)
dukkha-dukkha	unsatisfactoriness, pain, suffering
gocara-sampajañña	clear knowledge or understanding that there are just mental and physical processes
indriya	the five spiritual faculties: sati, samādhi, viriya, saddhā, and paññā
jhāna	meditative absorption
kāmacchanda	sensual desire
kamma	volitional action (of body, speech, and mind)
kāyānupassanā	contemplation of the body
khandha	five aggregates or categories: rūpa, vedanā, saññā, saṅkhāra, viññāṇa

kilesa	defilements, unwholesome qualities of the mind, any manifestation of greed, anger, and delusion (see lobha, dosa, and moha)
kusala (also see *akusala*)	kammically wholesome, skillful, profitable
lobha	greed, any kind of craving or liking (synonym for taṇhā)
magga-ñāṇa	path knowledge (leading to Enlightenment)
magga-phala	literally "path and fruit"; synonym for Enlightenment
mettā	loving-kindness, selfless love, unconditional love
mettā-bhāvanā	cultivation of loving kindness
micchā-diṭṭhi	wrong view
moha	delusion, ignorance, not understanding, not seeing reality (synonym for avijjā)
muditā	altruistic or sympathetic joy
nāma	mental processes, mind (collective term for vedanā, saññā, saṅkhāra, and viññāṇa)
nāma-rūpa	mental and physical processes
ñāṇa	synonym for paññā
nekkhamma	renunciation, "freedom from defilements"
nirodha	extinction

Pāli	name of the language in which the Buddhist scriptures (Pāli Canon) were first recorded
paññā	wisdom, understanding, knowledge, insight (synonym for ñāṇa)
paññatti	relative (conceptual) reality, concepts
paramattha	ultimate reality
pāramī	perfections, potential "talents": Perfection in giving, morality, renunciation, wisdom, energy, patience, truthfulness, resolution, loving-kindness, and equanimity
pariyutthāna	used to describe kilesas which arise in the mind
passaddhi	tranquility
pīti	joyful interest, enthusiasm, rapture
putthujjana	literally "one of the man folk," a worldling, someone who has not yet experienced Enlightenment
rūpa	physical processes, corporeality
sacca	truth (many meanings)
saddhā	faith, confidence, trust
samādhi	calmness, stillness or stability of mind
samatha	tranquility meditation, concentration meditation
saṃsāra	cycle of suffering, round of rebirths

sammā-samādhi	Right Samādhi
sammā-saṅkappa	Right Thought
sammā-sati	Right Awareness
sammā-vāyāma	Right Effort
samudaya-sacca	truth of the origin
saṅkhāra	mental formations
saṅkhāra-dukkha	the unsatisfactory nature of all existence, of all conditioned phenomena
saññā	recognition, memory, perception
sappāya-sampajañña	clear knowledge of suitability
sati	mindfulness or awareness
Satipaṭṭhāna Sutta	the four foundations of mindfulness, see kāyanupassanā, vedanānupassanā, cittānupassanā, and dhammānupassanā
sati-sambojjhaṅga	the enlightenment factor of mindfulness
sati-sampajjañña	mindfulness and clear comprehension
sātthaka-sampajañña	clear knowledge of whether a mental, verbal, or physical action is beneficial or not
sīla	morality, ethical conduct, virtue
somanassa	any kind of pleasant mental feeling, mental agreeable feeling, mentally pleasurable feeling

sukha	happiness
sutamayā paññā	wisdom or knowledge acquired through reading or hearing
sutta	discourse of the Buddha
taṇhā	synonym for lobha
upekkhā	a) neutral feelings and sensations (vedanā) b) equanimity, a wholesome mental state (saṅkhāra, cetasika)
vedanā	pleasant, unpleasant, or neutral feelings or sensations
vedanānupassanā	contemplation of feeling
viññāṇa	consciousness, cognition, the knowing mind
vipariṇāma-dukkha	the suffering in change
vipassanā	insight, insight meditation
viriya	effort, energy, "wisdom" energy, "remindfulness"
vītikkama	used to describe kilesas which are expressed verbally or physically
yoniso manasikāra	a) right attitude, right frame of mind, right attention b) wise consideration